Connected Code

The John D. and Catherine T. MacArthur Foundation Series on Digital Media and Learning

Engineering Play: A Cultural History of Children's Software, by Mizuko Ito

Hanging Out, Messing Around, and Geeking Out: Kids Living and Learning with New Media, by Mizuko Ito, Sonja Baumer, Matteo Bittanti, danah boyd, Rachel Cody, Becky Herr-Stephenson, Heather A. Horst, Patricia G. Lange, Dilan Mahendran, Katynka Martínez, C. J. Pascoe, Dan Perkel, Laura Robinson, Christo Sims, Lisa Tripp, with contributions by Judd Antin, Megan Finn, Arthur Law, Annie Manion, Sarai Mitnick, David Schlossberg, and Sarita Yardi

The Civic Web: Young People, the Internet, and Civic Participation, by Shakuntala Banaji and David Buckingham

Connected Play: Tweens in a Virtual World, by Yasmin B. Kafai and Deborah A. Fields

The Digital Youth Network: Cultivating New Media Citizenship in Urban Communities, edited by Brigid Barron, Kimberley Gomez, Nichole Pinkard, and Caitlin K. Martin

Connected Code: Why Children Need to Learn Programming, by Yasmin B. Kafai and Quinn Burke

The Interconnections Collection: Understanding Systems through Digital Design, developed by Kylie Peppler, Melissa Gresalfi, Katie Salen Tekinbaş, and Rafi Santo

Gaming the System: Designing with Gamestar Mechanic, by Katie Salen Tekinbaş, Melissa Gresalfi, Kylie Peppler, and Rafi Santo

Script Changers: Digital Storytelling with Scratch, by Kylie Peppler, Rafi Santo, Melissa Gresalfi, and Katie Salen Tekinbaş

Short Circuits: Crafting E-Puppets with DIY Electronics, by Kylie Peppler, Katie Salen Tekinbaş, Melissa Gresalfi, and Rafi Santo

Soft Circuits: Crafting E-Fashion with DIY Electronics, by Kylie Peppler, Melissa Gresalfi, Katie Salen Tekinbaş, and Rafi Santo

Inaugural Series Volumes

Six edited volumes were created through an interactive community review process and published online and in print in December 2007. They are the precursors to the peer-reviewed monographs in the series. For more information on these volumes, visit http://mitpress.mit.edu/books/series/john-d-and-catherine-t-macarthur-foundation-series-digital-media-and-learning.

Connected Code

Why Children Need to Learn Programming

Yasmin B. Kafai and Quinn Burke

The MIT Press
Cambridge, Massachusetts
London, England

First MIT Press paperback edition, 2016

MIT Press books may be purchased at special quantity discounts for business or sales promotional use. For information, please email special_sales@mitpress.mit.edu.

This book was set in Stone by the MIT Press. Printed and bound in the United States of America.

Library of Congress Cataloging-in-Publication Data

Kafai, Yasmin B.
Connected code : why children need to learn programming / Yasmin B. Kafai and Quinn Burke.
      pages   cm. — (The John D. and Catherine T. Macarthur foundation series on digital media and learning)
Includes bibliographical references and index.
ISBN 978-0-262-02775-5 (hardcover : alk. paper)—978-0-262-52967-9 (pbk.)
1. Computers and children. 2. Computer programming—Study and teaching (Secondary) 3. Scratch (Computer program language) 4. Constructivism (Education) I. Burke, Quinn, 1976– II. Title.
QA76.9.C659K34   2014
004.083—dc23
2014003658

10 9 8 7 6 5 4 3 2

To Seymour and for Nyla

Contents

Series Foreword

Digital media and networks have become embedded in our everyday lives and are part of how we engage in knowledge production, communication, and creative expression. Unlike the early years of computers and computer-based media, digital media are now commonplace and pervasive. Digital media have escaped the boundaries of professional and formal practice and the academic, governmental, and industry homes that initially fostered their development and have been taken up by diverse populations and noninstitutionalized practices, including the peer activities of youth. Although forms of technology uptake are diverse, a generation is growing up in an era when digital media are part of the taken-for-granted social and cultural fabric of learning, play, and social communication.

This book series is founded on the working hypothesis that those immersed in new digital tools and networks are engaged in an unprecedented exploration of language, games, social interaction, problem solving, and self-directed activity that leads to diverse forms of learning. These diverse forms of learning are reflected in expressions of identity, independence, and creativity and an ability to learn, exercise judgment, and think systematically.

The defining frame for this series is not a particular theoretical or disciplinary approach or a fixed set of topics. Rather, the series revolves around a constellation of topics investigated from multiple disciplinary and practical frames. The series looks at the relation between youth, learning, and digital media, but each contribution to the series might deal with only a subset of this constellation. Erecting strict topical boundaries would exclude some of the most important work in the field. For example, restricting the content of the series only to people of a certain age would mean artificially reifying an age boundary when the phenomenon demands otherwise. This would become particularly problematic with new forms of online participation where one important outcome is the mixing of participants of different ages. The same goes for digital media, which are increasingly inseparable from analog and earlier media forms.

The series responds to changes in our media ecology that have important implications for learning and that involve new forms of media literacy and modes of media participation. Digital media are part of a convergence between interactive media (most notably gaming), online networks, and existing media forms. Navigating this media ecology involves literacies that are being defined through practice but require more scholarly scrutiny before they can be incorporated into educational initiatives. Media literacy involves ways of understanding, interpreting, and critiquing media and also the means for creative and social expression, online search and navigation, and a host of new technical skills. The potential gap in literacies and participation skills creates new challenges for educators who struggle to bridge media engagement inside and outside the classroom.

The John D. and Catherine T. MacArthur Foundation Series on Digital Media and Learning, published by the MIT Press, aims to close these gaps and provide innovative ways of thinking about and using new forms of knowledge production, communication, and creative expression.

Foreword

Mitchel Resnick

I first met Seymour Papert more than thirty years ago. He was giving a talk at the West Coast Computer Faire, a free-spirited gathering of early personal-computer enthusiasts (in many ways, a forerunner of today's Maker Faires). In his talk, Papert presented a vision of a world in which computers would become an integral part of children's lives. He described how children would program computers to control robots, compose music, design games, develop simulations, and perform many other creative activities.

At the time, it was a bold, audacious dream, viewed by many as wildly unrealistic. Personal computers had just become available, and few children had access to them. But over the past three decades, many aspects of Papert's dream have become a reality. Millions of children around the world interact with computation in a wide variety of forms—electronic toys, mobile phones, game machines, laptops, and tablets. And they use computational devices to engage in a diverse range of activities, such as playing games, chatting with friends, exploring virtual worlds, and searching for information online.

At the same time, important elements of Papert's dream remain unfulfilled. Papert envisioned a world in which children would not only interact with premade computer applications but would design, create, and program with computational media—and, in the process, learn important problem-solving skills and project-design strategies.

What happened to Papert's dream? In the 1980s, there was initial enthusiasm for teaching computer programming (or coding) to children. Thousands of schools taught millions of students to code with Papert's Logo programming language. But the enthusiasm did not last. In most schools, the computer became a machine for delivering and accessing information, not a machine for making and creating. Most educators came to see computer programming as a narrow, technical activity that was appropriate for only a small segment of the population.

In *Connected Code: Why Children Need to Learn Programming*, Yasmin B. Kafai and Quinn Burke document the revival of Papert's dream. In the past few years, coding has suddenly become fashionable again, with numerous websites and organizations encouraging and supporting people to learn to code. My Lifelong Kindergarten research group at the MIT Media Lab has actively contributed to this trend, developing the Scratch programming language and online community to enable young people to program and share interactive stories and games, and collaborating with the Lego Company on the development of programmable robotics kits.

Kafai and Burke help put this coding revival in context. Although many people have focused on the job and career opportunities associated with computer programming (and those opportunities are indeed considerable), Kafai and Burke recognize that the appeal of coding goes beyond financial and economic motives. They situate the coding revival as part of the larger maker movement. I like to think of the coding revival as the coder movement. While the maker movement focuses on new ways for people to build, create, personalize, and customize physical things, the coder movement does the same for digital things. In both cases, the movements are catalyzed by both technological and cultural trends, as new technologies make it easier and cheaper to make (and code) things, and a cultural shift toward do-it-yourself activities broadens the range of people who want to be involved.

Perhaps the most important contribution of *Connected Code* is its introduction of computational participation as a guiding framework. In recent years, many researchers have rallied around computational thinking as a framework and motivation for computer science education, arguing that computational concepts can serve as a foundation for understanding all types of processes and systems in the world. I recognize the power and value of computational ideas but worry that computational thinking is often interpreted too narrowly, focusing on how individual people learn and use computational concepts for solving problems. Kafai and Burke's conception of computational participation serves as a broader, more inclusive framework for computer science education, expanding beyond individual problem solving to include personal expression, creative design, and social engagement. This shift, as Kafai and Burke note, has "implications for how programming is learned, what is designed, and where and how it is shared."

The ideas and stories in *Connected Code* provide hope for those of us who have spent many years trying to turn Papert's dream into a reality. We are heartened by the growing interest in the maker movement and coder movement. But we also recognize that these movements are in their infancies. New technologies for making and coding are spreading through society, but people's mindsets are slower to change. Too many people still view computers simply as tools for delivering and accessing information. My hope is that *Connected Code* will contribute to a broader culture change in which people develop new ways of thinking about computation and new ways of thinking about learning.

Acknowledgments

Writing a book that spans some thirty years of coding and education is a challenging enterprise, and many people have played pivotal roles along the way in shaping the ideas of this book and in providing feedback and support. Our first thanks goes to all of them, named or not named, because this book could not have been written without them.

Seymour Papert's ideas laid the foundation for how we think about learning, teaching, and computers. His papers and books, but in particular *Mindstorms: Children, Computers, and Powerful Ideas* (1980), were prescient in recognizing that education with computers was never about the devices themselves but ultimately about our own passions and our own desires to connect with each other. In addition, many discussions with Papert and his MIT Media Lab research group (of which one of the authors was a member) are the inspiration for this book. Seymour had a keen vision for what he imagined the future would be. Since his unfortunate accident in 2006, he has no longer had the opportunity to engage with computing and education as he once did, but we are confident that the recent comeback of coding would be a cause for celebration for him—as well as a confirmation of the educational theory of constructionism that he dedicated his career to advancing.

Long before Scratch, the research on Logo seeded many of the ideas around collaboration and coding that are prominent in today's networked youth communities. Members of the Epistemology and Learning Research group and then the Learning and Common Sense group at the MIT Media Lab continue to contribute to the conversations: Edith Ackerman, Aaron Brandes, Amy Bruckman, Idit Harel Caperton, Michele Evard, Aaron Falbel, Greg Gargarian, Ricki Goldman, Nira Granott, Paula Hooper, Jacqueline Karaslaanian, Fred Martin, Nicholas Negroponte, Steve Ocko, Michele

Evard Perez, Mitchel Resnick, Judy Sachter, Alan Shaw, Brian Silverman, Carol Sperry, Carol Strohecker, Hillel Weintraub, Uri Wilensky, as well as many teachers at Project Headlight, among them Gwen Gibson, Marquita Minot, principal Eleanor Perry, and Joanne Ronkin.

Special thanks go to Idit Harel Caperton, who pioneered software design for learning at the MIT Media Lab and whose support, ideas, and enthusiasm made it possible to develop this approach into game design for learning. She has now successfully extended this approach with Globaloria, a nationwide and award-winning program that engages children in entire schools and districts in creative computing.

Much of the research on understanding the peer pedagogy in children's collaborative programming continued at the University of California at Los Angeles with Sue Marshall and Cynthia Carter Ching as doctoral students. It is still one of the few longitudinal and comparative studies to date that has followed elementary schoolchildren as they collaborated in software design projects over several grade levels, moving from users to programmers and then to lead designers in their teams. For several years, Cathleen Galas, then a teacher, played an instrumental role in integrating programming activities into her science classroom, along with the administrative support of Deborah Stipek and Sharon Sutton at the Corinne Seeds University Elementary School.

For the development of and research on Scratch, collaborations with Mitchel Resnick's Lifelong Kindergarten group have been instrumental. Mitchel's dedication to keeping Scratch an open community is admirable as is his eloquence in capturing the successes of Scratch—both the site's growing number of projects and members and also the creative projects of the young Scratchers themselves. The work of many others from the Lifelong Kindergarten Group has played a key role in the development of this book and in the development of the Scratch programming language itself. This group includes Robbin Chapman, John Maloney, Amon Millner, Natalie Rusk, Elisabeth Sylvan, and more recently, Amos Blanton, Karen Brennan, Andrés Monroy-Hernández, and Ricarose Roque.

Many graduate students at UCLA played key roles in the early days of researching the implementation of Scratch at the Computer Clubhouses in Los Angeles, most notably Kylie Peppler in her extensive examination of digital media arts and learning with Scratch, along with Grace Chiu, Shiv Desai, and Jessie Mao, who documented the mentors' interactions. Thanks also to Natashka Jones and James Watson of the South Los Angeles Computer Clubhouse Youth Opportunities Unlimited for welcoming us into their neighborhood and community along with dozens of undergraduates as mentors.

In Philadelphia, Deborah Fields was one of the first to move Scratch from afterschool clubs into school classrooms, deepening our understanding of how people access online communities and how expertise is recognized in different communities. In the last five years, as the focus has shifted to the Scratch online community and collaborations, Deborah Fields has been key in designing and researching new opportunities for such collaborations both online and offline, together with Chad Mote, Eunkyoung Lee, and now Veena Vasudevan and the MIT Lifelong Kindergarten group. Deborah Fields has also led the way with Michael Giang and Nicole Forsgren Velasquez in understanding the different dimensions of participation in the larger Scratch online community. Many people in Philadelphia helped pave the way for this work in their schools and classrooms, among them Chris Lehman, Jeremy Spry, and Luke van Meter at the Science Leadership Academy.

We also wish to thank many others who have contributed at various stages to this book, among them Ann and Mike Eisenberg, Joanne Goode, Doreen Nelson, Keith Sawyer, Eliot Soloway, Orkan Telhan, and Sherry Turkle, for their various comments on and early encouragement on drafted chapters; Abi Luftig for her careful reading and copy edits on multiple drafts and page proofs as well as Barrie Adleberg and Veena Vasudevan for checking page proofs. On the other end, Mitchel Resnick and several anonymous reviewers provided valuable comments and feedback on the completed manuscript. Thanks as well to the many people who have helped with locating and contributing images from their archives for chapter illustrations, including Leah Buechley, Thomas Dunlap, Danny Edelson, Ann and Mike Eisenberg, Barry Hetherington, Ellen Hoffman, Sherry Hsi, Jacqueline Karaaslanian, Eunkyoung Lee, Mitchel Resnick, and Bo Sterne Thomson. Our book editors, first Katie Helke and then Susan Buckley, were two of our best supporters, always offering thoughtful and honest feedback as the manuscript evolved.

Our work would have not been possible without the support of the National Science Foundation, which over the last twenty years has generously funded (first with an Early Career Award to Yasmin Kafai and then with substantial collaborative grants to Yasmin Kafai and Mitchel Resnick's groups) the research studies whose cumulative insights are captured in this book. And although we have to add the customary disclaimer that any opinions, findings, conclusions, and recommendations expressed in this book are ours and do not reflect the views of the National Science Foundation, we are thankful for this instrumental support.

Finally, our friends and families have made room for writing in various ways. To our parents, who have forever been our strongest supporters, and to our friends and families, who have encouraged us and have been there over and over for us: this often tacit but always consistent support helped us see this project to an end. Thank you to Kay and, in particular, to Nyla, whose patience with Quinn was nothing short of herculean for a four-year-old who could not understand why her father had to stay inside working on the computer rather than joining her outside on the swings.

Yasmin B. Kafai and Quinn Burke

1 The Comeback of Coding

On June 23, 1990, The Computer Museum in Boston opened an exhibit featuring the world's first Walk-Through Computer. Fifty times the size of a desktop model, the computer was one of a kind. Visitors to the museum ran their hands across a keyboard with buttons the size of their heads, looked up at a motherboard the size of a score board, and measured their height against a floppy disk that met them at eye level. More than just a model, the computer ran a functional software program, allowing visitors to take a tour of the world on a mammoth screen. With a giant trackball to guide the cursor, visitors chose starting and destination points from among three hundred major world cities, and the program calculated the shortest land route between any two sites, displaying geographic sights that would be encountered from one locale to another. The exhibit was a success and received global press coverage. Thousands walked through the interior world of a device that could show them the world on a gigantic screen and whose enormous size seemed to comment on the computer's ever-growing presence in the world.[1]

A few miles from the museum, a different sort of exhibit was being held in a Boston public elementary school in what was then one of the city's poorest neighborhoods. Project Headlight featured the world's largest school computer lab with hundreds of computers. Part of a bold experiment sponsored by MIT's Media Lab, Project Headlight was likewise committed to getting users "inside" the inner workings of computers. Rather than a walking tour, however, the project put children into the veritable driver's seat behind the machines and taught them how to manipulate the computer's behavior by using the programming software Logo. Initiated by Seymour Papert, the project was founded on an idea that was unusual at that time—that children should (and could) program computers. Inside Project Headlight, the computers were arranged in circles in a large space near various classrooms rather than being closeted away into a single classroom. Once a day, students programmed stories, software, and games in Logo and sometimes exchanged them with children in other countries. Project Headlight was a great success for the years it lasted. Thousands of students and teachers were pioneers in bringing programming to the grade-school level and collectively provided a living example what learning and teaching with computers could look like.[2]

When The Computer Museum closed its doors in 1999 and moved across the Charles River to the Boston Museum of Science, the exhibits for the Walk-Through Computer were packed up and stored but never reassembled. The computers from Project Headlight were sent to individual computer labs because the open learning space for collaborative coding was deemed to be unfeasible within the traditional structure of the school day. A gigantic computer that people walked through? Schoolchildren who programmed computer games? Both ideas seemed to belong to the realm of infeasibility. In the second half of the 1990s, laptop devices became increasingly popular, and the notion of big machines seemed archaic. The development of

Figure 1.1
The Walk-Through Computer exhibit at The Computer Museum in Boston, 1994. Photo by Paula Lerner.

Figure 1.2
Project Headlight at a Boston elementary school, 1990. Photo by L. Barry Heatherington.

CD-ROMs (compact discs read-only memory) made the toil associated with coding seem equally archaic. Who wanted to bother with the laborious process of coding programs when the applications could be easily downloaded with the slip of a disk?

Yet both the giant Walk-Through Computer and Papert's coding circles were evidence of a belief in the potential for all of us—regardless of age or experience—to touch the machine itself, to get inside the inner workings of the computer, and to connect with our own passions through the machine. And now the pendulum is swinging back. Today the computer has moved out of museums and computer labs. Its presence is felt most deeply in the omnipresent hand-held and touch-screen devices that run digital applications tailored to the professional and social needs of the individual user. Computers—desktops, laptops, tablets, and mobile devices—have tangibly and personally become extensions of ourselves,[3] and coding, once solely the erudite pastime of techies, is now being recognized by educators and theorists as a crucial skill, even a new literacy, for all children.[4]

We often forget about the importance of the social, personal, and tangible elements that are associated with learning with, through, and about computers. Yet these elements play a fundamental role in helping us to understand the inner workings of the machine and the dynamics of contributing to social networks. In *Connected Code*, we examine the possibility of rediscovering the computer as a means for personal and social connectivity. Despite the initial enthusiasm for both The Computer Museum's exhibit and Papert's educational workshop, why did getting "inside" computers not become an educational priority for our schools, and how is programming now making a comeback?

Returning programming to schools is one response to a call to develop computational thinking in young learners. The premise is that by learning to think like a computer scientist, students can solve everyday problems, design systems that we all use in daily life, and progress and innovate in other disciplines.[5] *Computational thinking* has now become an umbrella term for computer science's contributions to reasoning and communicating in an increasingly digital world. Despite the emergence of computational thinking as a conceptual framing for teaching programming, however, the revival of programming is not being led by either educators or promoters of computational thinking.

One significant push for programming's resurgence has come from an unexpected source—the do-it-yourself (DIY) ethos that is characteristic of digital youth cultures. Computers now are accessible inside and outside of school, and children use their personal machines to innovate with technology by creating their own video games, interactive art projects, and even programmable clothes through electronic textiles. The same computers on which they create these homespun items also connect them to wider networks of other young users who share common interests and the commitment to "doing it ourselves" through a mutual DIY ethic. Schools may be able to incorporate some of the methods of these informal collaborative communities (particularly creative production and networked participation) in their own formal environments. These aspects of the DIY culture provide promising models for how schools can adapt their approaches to learning and teaching with computers in the digital age. And schools certainly have such a responsibility.

Despite the upsurge of DIY youth communities, these communities represent a small portion of the youth population.[6] Most children use their devices—whether laptop, iPad, iPhone, or Droid—to consume commercial media. Computers may have become extensions of ourselves, but to what extent are we teaching children how to design and manage these extensions? How do we help children become producers and not just consumers of digital media? What role should programming play in facilitating such production, and how can schools best help children to develop literacies for the twenty-first century? With the universal prominence of digital media, do we need to be concerned about equity issues of access and participation? Given that these questions involve individual identity, social well-being, and the wider economic viability of this country, we need to revisit the question of what it means to be literate in today's society. One way to do this is to return to the ideas that led Papert to establish computer coding circles in schools and situate these ideas in today's educational, cultural, and technological environments.

This first push to put programming in schools was inspired by Papert's 1980 book *Mindstorms: Children, Computers, and Powerful Ideas*, in which he argued that by programming computers, children could learn about mathematics, new topics such as cybernetics, and their own thinking (according to the progressive views of education promoted by John Dewey, Paulo Freire, and Maria Montessori). The book was controversial but also helped educators around the globe to see the value of having computers in schools. *Mindstorms* promoted a vision of computers in school that came alive through the coding circles of Project Headlight described in introductory vignette.

In *Connected Code*, we discuss what children are actually interested in programming, what contexts they do it in, and how they do it. Through the lens of the introductory programming language Scratch, we examine these connections between children and computer programming along several dimensions:

From code to applications, illustrating how students increasingly learn programming not as an abstract discipline but as a way to make actual applications, such as video games and digital stories;

From tools to communities, highlighting the shift from learning code as an individualistic endeavor to learning it as a social enterprise;

From scratch to remix, pointing to the growing possibilities and ethical challenges that are associated with repurposing code as a starting point (or from scratch) for programs; and

From screens to tangibles, showcasing how coding and computing have moved beyond stationary screens, reintroduced a tangible dimension to digital media, and allowed users to immerse themselves in the physical world through programmable toys, tools, and textiles.

Our book also explores the current developments in cloud learning, which captures this potential to compute collaboratively. As an individualistic view of computing evolves into one that focuses on the sociological and cultural dimensions of learning to code, computational thinking will expand to include social participation and personal expression. Computational participation, as we see it, is the ability to solve problems with others, design systems for and with others, and draw on computer science concepts, practices, and perspectives to understand the cultural and social nature of human behavior.

Introducing Computational Thinking

In 2006, computer science professor Jeannette Wing coined the term *computational thinking* in a short essay that was published in *Communications of the Association for Computing Machinery*, the monthly journal of the world's largest professional organization for computer scientists. She defined *computational thinking* broadly as all "aspects of designing systems, solving problems, and understanding human behaviors"[7] that highlight the contributions of computer science. She argued that understanding the world computationally gives a particular lens to understanding problems and contributing to their solutions. Computational thinking is often associated solely with computer science, but it applies computer science principles to other disciplines to help break down the constituent elements of any problem, determine their relationship to each other and the greater whole, and then devise algorithms to arrive at an automated solution. Computational thinking is not limited to mathematics and the sciences, and it does not necessarily involve the use of a computer.

Thinking computationally or like a computer scientist can help students better articulate and comprehend other disciplines. But Jeanette Wing provides several examples of how we already engage in computational thinking on a daily basis. When children sort and store Lego brick pieces, for example, they might start by sorting them according to particular criteria, such as "All rectangular thick blocks in one bin," "All thin ones in another," and so on. Computer scientists call this approach *hashing*. Most children (and adults) clean up large quantities of Lego bricks by dumping them into one big bucket. But suppose that the children want to build a bigger project with Legos and need to construct the project by selecting particular pieces in a set sequence. Rather than looking through a pile of hundreds of Legos every time a piece is needed, the children would be better served by having itemized compartments of bricks that are arranged by size, shape, and color. For the construction of ambitious and precise structures, establishing these compartments would significantly shorten search time and allow the builders to enjoy what they really wanted to do in the first place—build and not search.

Jeanette Wing's essay on computational thinking provoked a wide range of responses within the computer science community and beyond. Members of a discipline often begin to define its essence by discussing its core ideas and contributions. But the effects of computational thinking have reached far beyond the boundaries of academic computer science, and it has become a catch-all term for what understanding computer science can contribute to the increasingly digital world in which we live. These discussions on computational thinking also noted that technology courses that teach only word processing and presentation software do not engage students in the deeper analysis needed to think creatively and critically with digital media. They also made clear that most young people know little about computer science as a discipline or the ways that they can apply it to their own daily lives. In short, computational thinking has become the rallying cry for those who study what youth need to know about computer science and what it means to think systematically about solving all types of problems, big and small.

What might computational thinking (designing systems, solving problems, and understanding human behaviors) look like in schools, and how could we teach it? Two workshops meetings convened by the U.S. National Academy of Sciences set out to answer these questions and provide examples and various approaches to defining and expanding computational thinking and pedagogy.[8] In addition, several professional groups (such as the Computer Science Teachers Association and nonprofits like Shodor) have set out to make computational thinking accessible for children by aligning K–12 educational standards and curricular integration to core content subjects. Other supporting efforts include Google's launch of the Exploring

Computational Thinking website with links to Web resources and lesson plans for K–12 teachers in science and mathematics.[9]

Perhaps most surprising is the decision to teach computational thinking without computers, which alleviates the concerns of some computer scientists and Jeannette Wing herself, who wished not to equate computational thinking with programming in Java (or any one single programming language). The Computer Science Unplugged activities were developed by a group in New Zealand, and they exemplify the computerless approach, applying ideas in computing "through engaging games and puzzles that use cards, string, crayons and lots of running around." The activities are suitable for students from elementary school to high school.

Other approaches rely on computers, but like Computer Science Unplugged, they resist tying computational thinking solely to learning how to code. They have focused on introducing computational thinking to students by having them design digital applications that are personally meaningful to the designer. Most popular are game designs, the construction and coding of robotics, and the use of media filters to collect and organize news information for more efficient journalism. This focus on designing applications such as games, robots, and stories also connects well with computational thinking's general focus on designing systems, solving problems, and understanding human behaviors. Applications are designed for others to use, which means that designers have to consider human behavior as they design their systems and need to solve problems as they translate application ideas into code. For a K–12 audience, we like to think about it as computational participation because purpose, community, and practices are key.

Expanding to Computational Participation

Computational thinking has progressed since Jeannette Wing's 2006 article. What started as a concept now exists in curricula and pedagogy in K–12 schools and school-based clubs across the country.[10] Although computational thinking offers a framework for how to use technology more rigorously and critically in schools, there also remains the question of outcome. Teaching children to think more rigorously and critically is an admirable goal, but it is hardly a new one. Many curricula (in ancient Greece, philosophy and rhetoric; in the nineteenth century, Latin; and in the twentieth century, computer programming) were intended to develop more rigorous critical thinking. And despite the fact that many K–12 schools have had the machines for over thirty years, little progress has been made in programming education.

Those who would like to return programming to the schools need to articulate an argument that extends beyond the common desire to make children more rigorous thinkers. Learning how to think is an admirable goal, but it is a limited conception of what programming affords young learners. If programming is promoted solely as a more effective way to think (and not as an effective way to communicate logically and creatively), then we will again fail to understand what teaching and learning code can afford us in a networked age. Learning to code ultimately manifests its worth when it increases an individual's capacity to participate in today's digital publics. Programming is a form of expressing oneself and of participating in social networks and communities. In this book, we argue that computational thinking needs to be thought of as computational participation because the computer programs that are being created, used, repurposed, and shared have become our social connections. This view of code as connected has implications for how programming is learned, what is being designed, and where and how it is being shared.

The development of creative and critical networks to share information and ideas stands as the model for students who wish to create a more collaborative and open society. It is not enough to be "hanging out" on the computer and "messing around" on occasion, as media researcher Mizuko Ito and colleagues discuss in their 2009 book on youth engagement with digital media. Referring to a third category as "geeking out," Ito and her colleagues note that few youth engage in such activity and that such engagement with technology is rarely found in schools. Computational thinking represents schools' attempt to remedy this lack of engagement and provide children with the concepts and skills that will allow them to solve problems algorithmically. Computational participation focuses on the practices and perspectives that are needed to contribute within wider social networks, including but not limited to schools.[11] Within the wider network of creative and critical thinkers, educators have the chance to take the "geek" out of "geeking out" and set new academic and social norms for what it means to use technology meaningful.

When computation is thought of in terms of participation and not just thinking, it becomes clear that there is a tremendous discrepancy in who gets to participate. Most schools that have begun to address computational thinking in their programs serve children from upper-middle-income families. These students learn to think computationally because they have the opportunity to participate computationally. This has been the case for the last twenty years.[12]

Despite this history of inequity, the disparity in how children learn by engaging with computers has only recently been recognized as a wider sociocultural problem. Throughout the 1980s, study after study documented that schools in underresourced communities had far fewer computers than their suburban and private counterparts. Initiatives like Project Headlight, where computers were accessible to all, were rare. Leveling the playing field was less about how children best learn with computers and more about simply providing access to computers. In the 1990s, the focus was almost entirely on access to computers, not curricula or pedagogy, and initiatives such as "Net Day" were dedicated to bringing computers into school and connecting them to the Internet.

Although initiatives that addressed the "digital divide" accomplished much good, providing access to machinery tended to overshadow a systemic issue that media scholar Henry Jenkins called the "participation gap"[13]—children's usage of digital media in creative and critical ways. Debunking the notion that schoolwide access alone represented an equitable solution, technology educator Mark Warschauer compared two schools that had the same number of computers but were located in neighborhoods with starkly different household incomes. His findings indicated that other factors were as important, if not more important, as access. Although students had equal access to computers in both schools, teachers taught and students learned different things at the different schools. Students in the high-income neighborhood learned to work creatively with computers, and at times even programming, and students in the low-income community learned word processing and ways to operate the machinery.

The extent to which K–12 schools have made progress in learning with computers since the turn of the twenty-first century is questionable, although the education community has recognized that there is a participation gap on multiple levels. Even before the term *participation gap* gained popularity, education researchers Jane Margolis and Allan Fisher captured its presence among school gaps in terms of gender with the 2002 publication of *Unlocking the Clubhouse: Women in Computing,* which set out to find why few women were working in computer science. Margolis and Fisher studied middle and high schools that prepared students in computer science and interviewed female student applicants, asking them what initially drew them to the discipline, what helped them persevere, and what made them leave computer science. They found what they termed "a geek" culture that was often inaccessible and unwelcoming to newcomers who were not familiar with programming skills and knowledge.

Then they set out to change the culture of the computer science department because they realized that just bringing in students was not enough. They needed to create new curricula and pathways into computing and foster a mentoring community within the field at large. To "open the clubhouse," they needed to target the K–12 pipeline, which became the focus of Jane Margolis and colleagues' next book, *Stuck in the Shallow End: Education, Race, and Computing*, which examined the long history of racial discrepancy and bias in schooling and computing. What initially was an issue of a lack of women in computing expanded to an issue of a lack of people from minority and then lower-income groups, addressing equity issues in computing on an increasingly widening scale.

The near total lack of computational participation in any introductory technology-based coursework means that few students consider computer science principles or even encounter computer science at any point in their K–12 educations. Although there are over 42,000 high schools in the United States, only 2,100 offer an Advanced Placement computer science course.[14] In fact, the number of introductory computer science courses has decreased by 17 percent since 2005. Such a drop is inexcusable given the U.S. Bureau of Labor Statistics' consistent listing of computer science jobs as one of the fastest growing professions in the country, with over 4 million new positions expected to be available by 2020.[15] Gender and racial disparity in the computer science field represents another significant hurdle. Although women make up 56 percent of all Advanced Placement test takers, only 21 percent of those who took the AP computer science exam in 2011 were female. The national total of African American computer science test takers that same year was twenty-nine (less than 1 percent).

Participation in computing is more than just having access; it also involves the quality of what a child actually does with the computer. This issue extends beyond gender, racial, and socioeconomic equity. Even many schools in high-income communities remain entirely on the receiving end of computer screens and are unacquainted with how programming allows users to become multimedia creators themselves. This move from the digital divide (having access to computers) to the participation gap (knowing how to make things on the computer) has become the driving force toward to what we call computational participation.

The goal of this book is to conceptualize computation in schools so that it encompasses functionality (in terms of hard skills and practices) and the sociopolitical and personal contexts in which children use digital media. Functional purposes usually include the basic skills and concepts that are needed to participate in society, sociopolitical contexts include the reasons that these skills and concepts are relevant in society, and personal contexts include the ways that these skills and concepts build and maintain relationships. These various purposes describe the fundamental aspects of any literacy, whether reading and writing printed texts or using and programming digital media. They also make clear that talking about computational thinking requires an understanding of the basic concepts and skills that are situated within the cultural and personal contexts of learning and schooling.

The Scratch Story

Much of what we discuss in this book is the story of Scratch, a media-rich programming language for beginning programmers. As chapter 2 illustrates in greater depth, Scratch followed the footsteps of Logo as not just a programming language but also a tool for personal expression and knowledge transformation. In 2001, when Scratch was in an early development phase, Mitchel Resnick, John Maloney, and Natalie Rusk at the MIT Media Lab and Yasmin Kafai, then at UCLA, submitted a grant to the National Science Foundation based on the idea of developing a new programming language for young people who participated in the Intel Computer Clubhouse Network.[16]

After visiting many of the one hundred Computer Clubhouses in twenty countries, they observed that few programming cultures like the one envisioned by Papert had developed. In many Computer Clubhouses, the programming software package sat unopened on a bookshelf. But many youth manipulated images of popular icons using the often complex features of the Adobe Photoshop program. The music studio was an equally popular destination.[17]

The idea was to develop a programming language that builds on the media practices that already were favored by youth in their leisure time. This language would allow participants to make graphics, animations, and games. It would not be confined to a particular purpose, would provide a low entry threshold for beginners with no prior experience, and would be able to be scaled up to more complex projects. Scratch (its name a play on popular DJ practices of making and remixing music) moved away from the focus on mathematics and science that traditionally was associated with programming. It presented a visual point-and-click interface that allowed young programmers to "write programs" by placing together blocks of elements and structures (figure 1.3).

Central to Scratch's original design was a capacity to circumvent the frustrating syntactic errors that are characteristic of typing code. It allows users

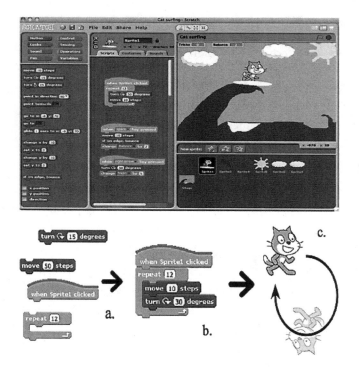

Figure 1.3

Two screenshots from the Scratch interface: a project entitled "Cat Surfing" (top) and a diagram showing the process of writing a basic coding script (bottom).

to use a mouse to drag and drop "bricks" of code onto a digital canvas. With knowledge of how to use a computer's mouse as the only prerequisite, children as young as eight years old were able to use Scratch to create their own programmable stories, games, and works of interactive art. Figure 1.3 shows such a creation—an encounter between an orange cartoon cat (Scratch's iconic character, called an object or a "sprite" within the program) and a huge wave. The interactive project utilizes sound effects, animation, and multiple forms of input to help the cat ride the wave to completion. "When Sprite clicked" (as illustrated in the second caption of figure 1.3) allows the player to flip the cat while on the surfboard. To create this individual movement, the designer of the interactive project selected a total of four bricks from the right side of the Scratch interface and combined or "stacked" them together to form a script within the left side of the screen, which, after being clicked, makes the cat turn 360 degrees on the Scratch screen.

Scratch has a rich library of programmable images or sprites, including the iconic Scratch cat figures. But the program's design also allows users to import images from the Internet, thus building on what youth in Computer Clubhouses do on their own. This capacity to bring in external images and sounds makes Scratch adaptable to young users' individual interests and helps them learn about the functionality of the program. For three years, Scratch was used and tested by a small group of Clubhouse members in Los Angeles and Boston who patiently worked with prototype after prototype, redoing their programs and providing us with instrumental feedback about what they liked to make and what was confusing.

What became apparent from these early exploratory sessions was that Clubhouse members loved finding an audience for their creations and regularly traded seats at their computers so that they could view and sample each other's work. Youth excitedly called out to each other across the room when they programmed a new feature or played their newly programmed games. It was clear that aside from readjusting the programming language, we needed to work on supporting collaboration and sharing of Scratch programs. When Andrés Monroy-Hernández, then a graduate student at the MIT Media Lab, created the online community where Scratch programs could be shared on the Internet, he called it "Scratchr," referencing the newly popular Flickr site where millions of people shared and annotated their own digital photos. At what eventually became Scratch.mit.edu, people were able to post and share their programs. The final version went public in May 2007 and features a simple "share" button that allows designers to click to upload a program to the Scratch site, which is hosted on a MIT server (figure 1.4).

Scratch's origin as a tool and its shift to a popular community speak to the wider shift from computational thinking to computational participation. Scratch users (or "Scratchers," as they are known on the website) found that the online community is as much a tool as the software itself (see

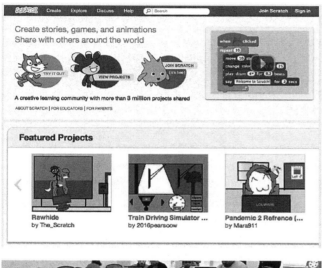

Figure 1.4
A screen shot of the Scratch Online Community portal (top) and a photo of a middle-school student experimenting with the video sensing feature of Scratch 2.0 on Scratch Day at the University of Pennsylvania, 2013. Photo by Darryl W. Moran Photography.

chapter 4). Being able to share ideas within the Forums sections, "friend" each other based on mutual interests, and remix others' work at the website are all fundamental tools by which to produce digital media (see chapter 5).

Scratch 2.0 has been in development for four years in the Lifelong Kindergarten Group at the MIT Media Lab. Following the shift from a tool to a participatory community, Scratch 2.0 blurs the division between the tool (Scratch as downloadable software) and the community (the online site). Users now are able to code and communicate at a single, cloud-based site. Likewise, to encourage participation, entirely new venues of creation extend beyond the screen. These include tangible construction kits that allow users to create their own interface (whether plastic, word, or any other material) and then hook up these homemade devices to program keys. Budding designers create their own touchpads and interface devices with alligator clips connected to conductive materials, including their own body (see chapter 6).

Although the story of Scratch is central to our book, it is representative of a larger trend. Programming languages such as Scratch are becoming more prevalent, but the do-it-yourself (DIY) movement has spurred an interest in making and producing technology artifacts. Today, youth both consume media (when browsing the Internet and sharing information on social networking sites) and produce content (when contributing to blogs and designing animations, graphics, and video productions). To map the participatory competencies that are needed in this new media landscape, Henry Jenkins and colleagues include creative designs, ethical considerations, and technical skills to capture youth's expressive and intellectual engagement with new media. More recently, these efforts to produce media have been associated with the growing maker movement and DIY movement, which involve arts, crafts, and new technologies. Educators should be especially interested in DIY communities, given the amount of time that youth spend in tackling highly technical practices, including film editing, robotics, and novel writing, among a host of other activities across various DIY networks.[18]

Overview

This book's eight chapters introduce key ideas of constructionism that were developed in Seymour Papert's *Mindstorms: Children, Computers, and Powerful Ideas* and of computational thinking, with illustrations of programming applications and activities. Before we launch into discussions of various applications of what we have termed computational participation, we revisit in chapter 2, Connected Learning, key tenets of constructionist learning as articulated by Papert through the development of Logo and now through Logo's successor, Scratch. We identify four dimensions characteristic of Constructionist thought (social, personal, cultural, and tangible), which are explored in chapters 3 through 6, illustrating the shift in how computer programming has evolved over the past two decades as a participatory process. Chapter 7, Connected Teaching, acts as a companion piece to chapter 2, by examining the teacher's side of constructionism. It explores what it means for teachers to transition into computation and collaboration, how they can create appropriate learning environments for their students, and what benefits and issues are associated with bringing do-it-yourself learning approaches into classrooms.

Between these two chapters that address the learning and teaching sides of constructionism, the four central chapters address the new social, personal, cultural, and tangible connections in teaching and learning programming. In chapter 3, From Code to Applications, we focus on the emergence of programming artifacts or applications as the focal point of learning. Learning programming once prized coding accuracy and efficiency as the signifiers of success. Today, however, rather than programming for the sake of programming, students can create authentic applications (such as games and stories) as part of a larger learning community. We present different examples of game designs, digital storytelling, and animations that showcase how applications situate the learning of key programming concepts and skills in different contexts.

In chapter 4, From Tools to Communities, we argue that learning to program is no longer performed as an isolated endeavor but is accomplished within a shared social context, utilizing open software environments and mutual enthusiasm to spur participation. The qualities of these shareable artifacts (a highly playable game, a sophisticated animation, or a particularly nuanced digital story) foster camaraderie and offer entry into coding communities. This chapter examines the emergence of youth programming communities and the ways that young designers enter and participate in such communities.

In chapter 5, From Scratch to Remix, we examine the emergence of new practices of participation and codesign as programming becomes a communal networked activity. Whereas programs once had to be created "from scratch" on a blank screen to demonstrate competency, seamless integration via remixing is the new social norm for writing programs. This certainly presents ethical challenges—particularly in the context of schools and their conception of plagiarism—but remixing also offers new networks for participation.

In chapter 6, From Screens to Tangibles, we look at how designers have moved coding and computing beyond stationary screens to the physical world through programmable toys, tools, and textiles. We start by examining stories about Lego Mindstorms kits, which helped popularize robotics learning in competitions in schools across the world before turning to new developments, such as electronic textiles and circuit construction kits.

Following chapter 7, we end with chapter 8, Coding for All, which sums up our insights and implications for introducing computational thinking and participation in K–12 classrooms and afterschool programs.

2 Connected Learning

Before I was two years old I had developed an intense involvement with automobiles. I was particularly proud of knowing about the parts of the transmission system, the gearbox, and most especially the differential. I loved rotating circular objects against one another in gear-like motions and, naturally, my first "erector set" project was a crude gear system. I found particular pleasure in such systems as the differential gear, which does not follow a simple linear chain of causality since the motion in the transmission shaft can be distributed in many different ways to the two wheels depending on what resistance they encounter. I believe that working with differentials did more for my mathematical development than anything I was taught in elementary school. Gears, serving as models, carried many otherwise abstract ideas into my head.

A modern-day Montessori might propose, if convinced by my story, to create a gear set for children. Thus every child might have the experience I had. But to hope for this would be to miss the essence of the story. I fell in love with the gears. This is something that cannot be reduced to purely "cognitive" terms. Something very personal happened, and one cannot assume that it would be repeated for other children in exactly the same form. My thesis could be summarized as: What the gears cannot do the computer might. The computer is the Proteus of machines. Its essence is its universality, its power to simulate. Because it can take on a thousand forms and can serve a thousand functions, it can appeal to a thousand tastes.[1]

In his now iconic "The Gears of My Childhood," the preface to *Mindstorms: Children, Computers, and Powerful Ideas*, Seymour Papert talks about how he made personal and emotional connections to gears, how they helped him to understand mathematics, and how the computer might become "gears" for other children. He notes that his personal experiences cannot be replicated by giving every child a gear set and that learners have to construct their own gears. He argues that the protean quality of the computer could allow it to become a universal construction material for learners to design and build objects. Rather than turning computers into teaching machines, children themselves would become programmers of the machine. This unexpected and bold proposal was driven by the belief that learning is constructed in the mind and heart and is connected to experiences in the world. Connected learning examines how the computer should be thought of as a tool for knowledge transformation, personal expression, and social relevance so that it allows learners to create and connect with others.

Papert viewed learning as the process of creating artifacts of personal and social relevance, connecting old and new knowledge, and interacting with others.[2] This description does not refer only to computers. Instead, it outlines the learning process and its conditions, and places a primacy on artifacts, the objects or "gears" that we construct and the personal meaning that we assign to them. Some have argued that this view of learning is too mindcentric, but it is equally sociocentric by including social relevance. The objects in our mind do not exist in isolation from our social worlds. In fact, they are closely grounded in and connected to the communities that we live in and the things that are valued by their members. In the 1980s, computers were still costly and available to only a few people. But digital media now are more affordable and portable and have moved into our daily lives. One of the objectives of this book is to examine how participation, collaboration, and computation can help young people learn and live in a digital world.

In this chapter, we examine the personal, social, cultural, and tangible dimensions of connected learning and their meaning for the design of learning opportunities, technologies, and environments. Papert, like Jean Piaget, saw learning as building knowledge structures,[3] but he added an important dimension: the artifacts of the mind have to move into the public world, where they can be examined, shared, and valued by others. In many ways, this view was prescient of the vast and distributed networks of digital objects and communities that comprise the Internet. It reflects the foundation for doing, thinking, and interacting—in short, learning—with any medium.

The personal, social, cultural, and tangible dimensions of connected learning are as relevant today as they were thirty years ago. They provide a foundation for understanding learning in a computational culture that values participation in terms of both production and connectivity. One of the "evocative objects" (to use Sherry Turkle's term)[4] for thinking about these issues is the programming language Logo,[5] which fueled many discussions about programming and computers in schools and putting children and not computers in charge of their learning.

Programming Tools, Programming Worlds

Logo was not the first and only programming language used by children. The programming languages Basic and later Pascal were equally prominent in many schools, and there was considerable debate about which programming language was best for schools. But in contrast to Basic and many other programming languages, Logo promised to offer more than just learning about programming: it taught mathematics, cybernetics, and science in new ways and also provided a pedagogy. These additions made Logo unlike any other programming language and became the precursor to Scratch.

In the late 1960s and early 1970s, most young programmers were writing program text by manipulating arrays of numbers or symbols. But in Logo, they wrote programs by moving a graphical object, called the "turtle," on the screen. Programming in Logo meant programming the turtle (figure 2.1). For instance, a programmer gave commands for the turtle to "move forward 10 steps and then turn 90 degrees to the right," which in Logo

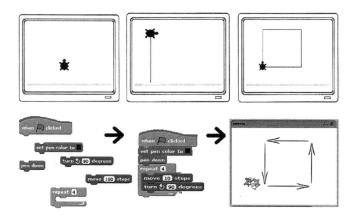

Figure 2.1

Screenshots for code written in Logo (top) and in Scratch (bottom). The Logo screenshot shows a turtle that is in a starting position and ready to be programmed in Logo. In the middle screen, the turtle has been programmed to execute the following steps: PEN DOWN FORWARD RIGHT TURN 90. The right screenshot shows a square that has been drawn by having the turtle repeat the commands four times or REPEAT 4 [FORWARD 90 RIGHT TURN 90]. The panel below shows individual Scratch programming blocks on the left, which are then combined and activated in the middle, resulting in the cat's movement on the Scratch stage at the right.

would be "FORWARD 10 RIGHT 90." The turtle then moved on the screen and provided visual feedback about the successful (or unsuccessful) execution of the programming steps. In addition, the turtle carried a pen that could leave a trace of its steps. When the command "PEN DOWN FORWARD 10 RIGHT 90" was executed four times, the drawing of a square appeared on the computer screen.

Today, Scratch continues Logo's idea of providing a programmable object, replacing the turtle with the orange cartoon Scratch cat. The most significant difference between Logo and Scratch is not each language's iconic mascots but how Scratch allows budding programmers to use snapable bricks rather than text to create movement, animation, and sound on the screen. The bottom of figure 2.1 demonstrates the same operation as the preceding Logo example, again using the pen, basic movements, and 90 degree turns, all of which are repeated (or "looped") four times to make a square. Whereas Logo's coding sequence is typed, however, Scratch users select composite bricks of code, stack them, and then let them create the sequence on the stage itself in the third panel.

Scratch's capacity extends far beyond the drawing of geometric figures, but the Scratch bricks and the stacking method are a better metaphor for "building" than typing code is. Logo introduced the notion of object-oriented programming into education, and Scratch took it to another level. In fact, most of today's professional programming languages have become object-oriented as well. A method that once was thought of as appropriate only for kids has turned out to be an intuitive (and often more efficient) way for adults to program.

Papert's vision extended beyond making programming more intuitive. He conceived of Logo as being more than just another programming language and ultimately saw it as an embodied learning world where users could experiment with ideas in science, mathematics, and cybernetics.[6] NetLogo and StarLogo, for example, have expanded Logo to run massively parallel programs on the computer: hundreds if not thousands of turtles can function simultaneously and interact with each other. These versions of Logo create microworlds for complex systems, helping learners to understand how unique complex behavior patterns can emerge from the overlapping interactions between many simple objects. Rather than watching and interacting with complex systems that were designed by others, learners can better understand such relationships by programming such simulations and designing computer games, animated stories, and robots (described in chapter 4).

In learning to write code, children can learn to articulate procedures, recognize repetition, and "debug" their own thinking when programs do not run as expected. These are the key features of computational thinking. Learning to program, learning to understand new ideas, and learning to learn are seen as inseparably linked.[7] In *Connected Code*, we see programs as commanding the machine and also as becoming the "objects-to-think-and-share-with" that can make learning personally, socially, culturally, and tangibly relevant and thus lead to computational participation. In the following sections, we outline these four elements of connected learning as they apply to learning to code.

Personal Dimensions

Today it is acknowledged that learners carry a rich set of informal ideas and theories that are connected to personal experiences. These funds of knowledge connect them with different medias and literacies in their communities. Learning is seen as a process of constructing knowledge and developing competencies in participation.[8] Papert saw knowledge construction as "the deliberate part of learning [that] consists of making connections between mental entities that already exist; new mental entities seem to come into existence in more subtle ways that escape conscious control.... This suggests a strategy to facilitate learning by improving the connectivity in the learning environment, by actions on cultures rather than on individuals."[9]

When students engage with Logo programming, they construct knowledge. This is what Papert termed "appropriation": learners make knowledge their own and begin to identify with it personally. The idea of constructing one's own knowledge draws heavily from Piaget's theory of knowledge development and his insight that children and adults understand the world in fundamentally different ways. Piaget identified two mechanisms, assimilation and accommodation, that explain how children as learners make sense of the world they interact with and integrate these experiences into their understanding. Connected learning builds on these mechanisms and focuses on the processes that help learners link to things that they already know.

These connections or appropriations go beyond the intellectual and add emotional values (as the gears did for Papert). Objects or artifacts play a central role in this process. Papert coined the term "objects-to-think-with" for objects in the physical and digital world (such as programs, robots, and games) that can become objects in the mind for constructing, examining, and revising connections between old and new knowledge (more about this in chapter 3). "Objects-to-think-with" (such as the Logo turtle) are particularly effective at supporting appropriation because they facilitate the learners' identification with the object. By designing a program or game (or its procedures, algorithms, and data structures), the personal knowledge becomes public and can then be shared with others.

Thinking about programs as personal objects that can be shared publicly is also occurring in Internet culture, which amasses personal items (such as photos, stories, and designs), introduces them in an massively wide public sphere, and allows them to take on entirely new meanings. In this context, computational thinking becomes computational participation because when code is created, it has both personal value and value for sharing with others. The "objects-to-think-with" in code are not just relegated to the mind but also are shared with others, thus adding social and cultural dimensions to the personal.

Social Dimensions

Learning is a social process, whether it occurs face to face or in the networked commons. Education researchers Jean Lave and Etienne Wenger's seminal 1991 work on apprenticeship learning stresses the communal nature of learning that often is missing in the focus on individual work that is characteristic of traditional schooling. More recently, gaming researcher Jim Gee has identified the importance of affinity cultures that are formed in gaming communities and the ways that this alternative learning environment offers an important lens by which to reevaluate schooling. In all learning communities, effective participation requires learners to search out, organize, and distribute responsibilities by collaborating with others as they engage in activities or create artifacts together. The collaborative agency that is required of learners emphasizes the active role that learners take in constructing community that builds knowledge and also designs artifacts that can be shared with others.[10] The proverbial "objects-to-think-with" become "objects-to-share-with," representing products and ethos of collaboration and learning in the communities.

The social dimensions of connected learning have focused on communities because personal construction of programs happens not in a vacuum but in a social context. Papert's research into Brazilian samba schools encapsulates his sense of social norms and interactions as being pivotal to any form of learning:

These are not schools as we know them; they are social clubs with memberships that may range from a few hundred to many thousands. Each club owns a building, a place for dancing and getting together.... During the year each samba school chooses its theme for the next carnival, the stars are selected, the lyrics are written and rewritten, and the dance is choreographed and practiced. Members of the school range in age from children to grandparents and in ability from novice to professional. But they dance together and as they dance everyone is learning and teaching as well as dancing. Even the stars are there to learn their difficult parts.[11]

Learning cultures can be neighborhood centers or even virtual worlds. The Intel Computer Clubhouse Network is an example of the former, with over a hundred locations worldwide where young people voluntarily gather to work with creative software applications to produce digital graphics, music, and videos. Unlike schools, the Computer Clubhouse does not follow a set curriculum, and members introduce each other to new activities with the support of coordinators and mentors. These ideas have also provided blueprints for virtual communities such as MOOSE Crossing, which allowed members program and share their virtual creations (more about this in chapter 4), and ClubZora, which facilitated discussions around values. Today's examples include virtual environments such as the Scratch community (with 1 million projects and hundreds of thousands of users) and the animation website Newgrounds (with a community of over 2 million members who have developed and shared over 500,000 Flash-based animations and video games). In all of these examples—Brazil's scattered samba schools, the network of Computer Clubhouses, and virtual communities— is a rich set of interactions between community members, developed from the ground up and governed through mutual interests and shared values.[12] Computational participation in this context is as much about socializing as it is about contributing in terms of valued artifacts, expertise, and feedback.

Cultural Dimensions

Connected learning also focuses on the cultural dimensions of learning— the politics that determine how particular ways of knowing, viewing, or doing are valued over others. And nowhere is this more important than in technology cultures, where, as Sherry Turkle and Seymour Papert have articulated, there are preferred ways of working with technologies that value the formal over the concrete. By studying and interviewing programmers, Turkle and Papert revealed that the officially promoted top-down planning approach is not always superior to a more improvised, bricoleur style approach. The bricoleur style is not a more advanced form of knowledge construction but is a different way of organizing planning and problem solving. Turkle and Papert argue for an epistemological pluralism, meaning that the bricoleur style (which favors concrete thought) can be as advanced as abstract thought, and they observe that among the sciences, computer science prizes abstract thinking.[13]

Learning by connecting knowledge and relationships also highlights other distinctions that society has drawn between critical thinking (traditionally understood as conceptually and linguistic based) and physical making (goal-based material work). In providing opportunities to concretize knowledge by creating material objects that embody ideas, we highlight ways that two modes of engagement with the world (that are usually held separate) can be reconnected. By encouraging the externalization of knowledge, we promote seeing the knowledge object as a distinct "other" with which we can enter a relationship that consists of questions that makers ask themselves about how the external object connects to other bodies of knowledge.[14] Understanding the boundaries and values that have been associated with such forms of engagement is critical to understanding who and how learners can connect with them. In other words, how we come to think and participate computationally is introduced and prescribed through cultural preferences.

Epistemological pluralism in connected learning thus is about how programs are designed, how problems are viewed, what values are reflected in artifacts, and how this can provide a context for learners to connect and engage with the practices in the field. Today the reevaluation of the concrete is displayed in the interest of young people in learning programming apps and other digital artifacts. This enthusiasm among youth for tinkering with source code has been a fundamental lever in the open-source movement, which aims to make technology development and interactivity more explicit, and argues that hiding relationships in these domains ultimately stifles collaboration and creativity. The ethos of the open-source movement of digital technology now has merged with that of the wider "can do" and communal sentiments of DIY culture, exemplified by craft activities, arts, and home repair.

Tangible Dimensions

Finally, the tangible dimension of constructionist learning brings back a physical dimension of learning and knowing that often is lost in the digital world. Consider the commands that move the Logo turtle one step forward and one degree to the right and that repeat this procedure 360 times: REPEAT 360 [FORWARD 1 RIGHT 1]. With the pen down, these commands draw a circle on the screen. A child could use his own body to pretend to be the turtle and thereby could execute every one of these steps. Papert called this feature *syntonic learning* because it allowed children to identify with computational objects in multiple ways:

For example, the turtle circle is *body syntonic* in that the circle is firmly related to children's sense and knowledge about their own bodies. Or it is *ego syntonic* in that it is coherent with children's sense of themselves as people with intentions, goals, desires, likes and dislikes.... One can also see it as *cultural syntonic* in that when drawing the circle, the turtle connects the idea of an angle to the idea of navigation which is closely rooted in children's extracurricular experiences.[15]

Both the Logo turtle and the Scratch cat allow children to manipulate objects on the screen as they would manipulate them in the physical world. The screen artifact sits "betwixt and between the world of formal systems and physical things; it has the ability to make abstract concrete ... by the same time it makes it visible, almost tangible and allows a sense of direct manipulation."[16] Although Turkle and Papert made this reference to objects on the computer screen, the inferences apply even more so to tangible artifacts that are part of the physical world. Early designs of the Lego/Logo construction kit extended the connection between the virtual screen world of Logo to the tangible world of Lego blocks. Students built robots with motors and gears and also designed programs to control activities and interactions.

The Walk-Through Computer described at the beginning of chapter 1 exemplifies this tangible dimension to an extreme. Its enormous floppy drive, monitor, and trackball made transparent the functionality of the computer and its software. Today's digital devices have moved away from the keyboard to interfaces and made interaction accessible to young and old alike. There also has been a shift from the massive Internet to individual applications, signifying a trend to smaller, personal applications. Although use and access are important, so also is understanding the functionality of these devices. Just as the Walk-Through Computer provided a glimpse into the innards of the machine, when programmability is extended to the physical world, it reveals that this world is programmable and malleable and thus controllable.

Connecting Construction, Code, and Culture

The personal, social, cultural, and tangible dimensions of connected learning reveal that learning is not solely a technical matter of skills to be mastered. When people are learning to code, the technical component may be the least problematic. As Caitlin Kelleher and Randy Pausch recognize in their analysis of introductory programming initiatives, the social and cultural barriers to learning programming are often "harder to address than mechanical ones because they are harder to identify and some cannot be addressed through programming systems"[17] alone. Programming is not just a cognitive skill that is used to design code. It also is a social and cultural skill that is used to participate in groups.

Our arguments for connected learning move beyond programming to examine how technology works and how design can incorporate a broader range of materials as more aspects of daily life move into the digital domain. The goal is to design both learning technologies and environments that provide the person and not the computer with agency.[18] There is a constant tension between agency (what learners do) and structure (how the context is constrained). From a connected learning perspective, the more freedom that teachers offer learners, the more they need to think about the boundaries of the established learning environment. Conversely, the more rules that initially are established, the more teachers need to think about what individual learners bring to the situation in terms of their interests, knowledge, and values. The key to good teaching is finding this balance between structure and agency, which is the great challenge of education in all its forms. On the one hand, educators need to distinguish between the roles of teacher and student. On the other hand (and paradoxically), this distinction must be blurred so that both teacher and student are unified as learners. Likewise, cultural context, practices, and perceptions play a critical role in making connections among what is being learned, how it is being learned, and who should learn it. Although these dimensions of connected learning are less tangible than other aspects, they are nonetheless key in understanding why computation has had such a difficult time taking roots in K–12 and why it is being promoted again today.

This theoretical chapter focuses on the commonality that all individuals share as learners, and chapter 7 examines the teacher's side of connected learning. In other chapters, we expand on various dimensions by illustrating how the programming of applications (chapter 3) can generate personal relevance and how an authentic audience (chapter 4) can provide support and feedback in ways that are unlike how children experience these things at school, at home, and with their peers. We also recognize that these communities come with certain mindsets, values, and histories. Nowhere is this more apparent than in the digital culture, where issues about equity and participation have been critical. Finally, we create artifacts that are visible and tangible signs of our participation (chapter 6). This is perhaps the most complicated relationship in learning, particularly because in a digital culture, most participation and production take place on the screen. By reevaluating the concrete as a mode of thinking and a form of digital production, we highlight a learning that is about objects to be made, to be thought with, and to be shared with others.

3   From Code to Applications

It's Wednesday afternoon at the Hennigan Elementary School in Boston. In a large and open area of Project Headlight, 17 fourth-grade students and their teacher are grouped around two large circles, each composed of a dozen or so desktop computers. Debbie sits at her computer swinging her legs, her hands poised over the keyboard, completely absorbed in her programming project. To her right, Naomi programs letters on the computer screen in different colors and sizes. Next to her, Michaela debugs a program for a mathematical word-problem involving fractions, comparing thirds and halves by using a representation of measuring cups that are filled with different amounts of orange juice and water. She is very involved with her design, typing with one hand while the other touches the shapes on her computer monitor. A few computers away, the teacher is trying out Tom's program, talking with him about one of his explanations of "what mixed fractions are." In the background, Charlie walks around the second circle, holding his notes in one hand and chewing on a pencil. He stops suddenly at Sharifa's computer. He chats with her for a moment, presses a key or two on her keyboard, and watches Sharifa's designs as they appear on the computer screen. After looking at her programming code, moving the cursor up and down on the screen, he calls out, "Hey Paul, come see Sharifa's program. It's a fractions clock!" The noise and movement around the computer area do not seem to bother the students. Back at the other circle, Naomi has completed the title screen for her piece of software, which reads "Welcome to Fractions Land! by Naomi." She stretches her arms and looks around to see what is new in her friends' programs. She then leans over towards Debbie and asks what she is doing.[1]

Learning fractions typically elicits less excitement from fourth-grade students and their teachers. Yet creating real-world scenarios for fractions and explaining their meanings through function rather than just description makes for richer—and more personally relevant—learning, on and off the computer.[2] Project Headlight was unique because it incorporated mathematics into digital media design and also because fourth-grade students were creating such media themselves through the direct application of ratios and division. And rather than simply submitting their work to their teacher for a letter grade (which they always had done in the past), the fourth-graders were creating digital games and simulations for a more authentic audience—the third-grade students at their school, whose first encounter with fractions would be based on the older students' ingenuity and industriousness in designing with computers.

This was an unusual scene for another reason. Students were learning programming in schools without necessarily realizing that they were learning programming. Rather than learning about code by listening to lectures and doing drills with conditionals, loops, and variables, students were learning about programming code by designing their own software applications. Rather than sequestering themselves in a computer lab once a week, the students were working both individually and communally on their fraction designs every day of the week. And rather than sitting in front of a screen answering fraction questions, students were becoming instructional designers for other students. In educational technologist Idit Harel Caperton's innovative conception of the instructional software design project, programming class and mathematics class become inextricably intertwined: computing and mathematics can no longer be perceived as anything but overlapping, mutually informing disciplines.[3] But perhaps more significantly, Caperton's K–12 intervention demonstrated an even more fundamental, if tacit, intertwine—the overlap between learning to code and learning to create with computers.

In the 1980s, when programming was first introduced on the K–12 level, students usually participated once or twice a week for an hour at a time. These isolated moments of coding existed within a computer lab, and after the session, students returned their "normal" classes. Learning to program was about learning to write code, develop algorithms, and design data and control structures, and it resulted in functional, if not necessarily efficient, programs. Hundreds of studies document these early efforts, reviewing what students need to learn about syntax, control structures, conditionals, recursion, data structures, and variables and what related challenges arise when teaching programming to young learners.[4]

Although much planning and problem solving went into writing programs at this time, critics claimed that there was little empirical evidence demonstrating what students were learning in terms of programming and whether such learning transferred to planning and problem solving.[5] Logo was an inspired first step in introducing coding, but its lack of integration into K–12 core subject content eventually helped undermine its popularity in K–12 schools. Whatever initial excitement children may have experienced with programming computers, the lack of connection to wider subject matter meant that they were not motivated to persist with the software after the early enthrallment wore off. Most teachers were unaware of the potential of code to support and expand subject-matter content, and they typically viewed such technology as an eclectic elective within the school rather than a means to ground and support core content mathematics and science learning.[6]

Designing applications rather than programming code responded to these criticisms of programming research and Logo. In an extensive review of the research on K–12 programming instruction, education researcher David Palumbo[7] independently came to the same conclusions that Caperton arrived at with the design of the instructional software project: the teaching and learning of programming need to be integrated with regular class work and other subject matters, provide a context for explanations, and foster personal relevance among students. In fact, the criticisms directed toward programming and specifically Logo—lack of sufficient time, complexity, and personal applicability—could be leveled against many other curricular activities in school, not just programming. What and how students were learning in school and how it connected to their learning outside of school emerged as a central topic of discussion in computer programming and in education in general during the late 1980s and early 1990s.[8]

Most prominent in these discussions was a push for authenticity in learning.[9] One meaning for *authenticity* is that what learners encounter in the classroom corresponds to what professionals do in the field itself. In terms of programming, this means that students in school should not encounter coding purely as an abstract discipline but instead should learn how experts in the domain approach the topic to create real applications. A second component is personal authenticity, and it relates to recognizing the personal interests and funds of knowledge that children bring to school. What are kids interested in creating? What is meaningful to them in terms of making their lives more efficient, more fun, and more interesting? The third component—authentic audiences—builds on this need for relevance, prompting children to make products of learning that are meaningful to each other, not just the teacher. Finally, the fourth authenticity is designing for real-world audiences, which prompts genuine feedback and meaningful and translatable assessment.

This focus on authenticity aligned digital media design practices with the wider shift among educators from 1980s onward. The goal was to create contexts in and around schools that promote open-ended forms of problem solving and situate learners so that they can create personally and socially meaningful applications.[10] This shift came to even greater fruition with the new millennium and the arrival of Web 2.0.[11] The current opportunities to create and socialize through digital media have increased with an ever-growing range of software applications. Making and sharing online are no longer purely technical skills but are increasingly social skills, and computer programming has again returned to schools not as an eclectic technology course but as a literacy skill. Considering this, what role do application-driven pedagogy and curricula play in ensuring that programming fares better today than it did thirty years ago? What software applications can schools leverage to make programming more palpable and practical to both students and teachers? And last, what kinds of software applications are children programming on their own, and how can educators create new and improved contexts for such creative coding? These questions are the focus of this chapter.

Designing Software Applications for Learning Coding

With this new push for authenticity on multiple levels, Caperton's research through Project Headlight represents a new standard for teaching children that computer programming can produce meaningful software applications. As mentioned in this chapter's opening vignette, Debbie and her classmates designed instructional fraction applications for younger students in their school:

Debbie shows Naomi her programming code. "It's a long one," she says, running the cursor down the screen, very proud of the 47 lines of code she has programmed for her "HOUSE" procedure [figure 3.1]. She then exits the LogoWriter editor to run her program for Naomi, who moves her chair closer to Debbie's. In a slow, quiet voice, pointing to the pictures on the screen, Debbie explains to Naomi: "This is my house scene. I designed all these shapes; each one equals one half. In the house, the roof has two halves, the door has two halves, and I will add to this scene two wooden wagons and a sun. I'll divide them into halves too.... The halves, the shaded parts, are on different sides of the objects. You know, you can use fractions on anything. ... Do you like the colors?"

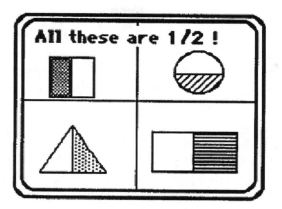

MARCH 23, 24

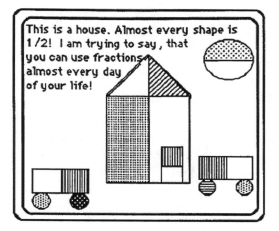

Debbie's final "House Scene"

Figure 3.1
Screen designs of Debbie's fraction house. Reprinted with permission.

In this anecdote, fourth-grader Debbie has put fractions to practical use, but for the two girls, the object—the house, the scene itself—is the focal point of the girls' exchange, not the fractions. Although concerns over the house's color scheme are irrelevant, the aesthetics of the house are inseparable from the geometry of the house. To establish meaning—at least, initially—the focus needs to be on the whole rather than the constituent elements. The house gives Debbie a way to talk about math and Naomi a way to see math. Together, along with the coding, talking and seeing also constitute computational participation. Through the object, learners grasp a way to think, connect, and communicate. Debbie's house also illustrates personal appropriation. This was a dramatic shift in Debbie's relationship to fractions. At the beginning of class, she and others seemed uninterested in the project, and she seemed to go through the motions of creating worksheet-like exercises in her program. But the house scene changed her attitude, partly because of the recognition that she received from classmates for her original design. For Debbie, the design and creation of the house demonstrated her knowledge of fractions and also gave her an object by which she could meaningfully demonstrate her knowledge to her own peers. As Papert explains, "The shifts in Debbie's thinking were not just a matter of knowing facts and skills. Her phrase 'you can put them [i.e. fractions] on top of anything' showed an epistemological shift and an epistemological intention. She made a shift from one kind of knowledge (formal, teacher knowledge) to another kind of knowledge (personal, concrete, her own)."[12] Debbie's project made fractions real to her and to her audience (Naomi, her other classmates, and the third-graders). Previously, fractions had existed only in classrooms, and even within those narrow confines, they were further restricted to the confines of the teacher's blackboard and to Debbie's worksheets. "Do you like the colors?" she asks Naomi about the fractions— not "Is this right?" or "Can you check if this is correct?" The fractions are fully, intimately hers.

Papert also notes of Debbie that "one day she realized that the programming technique she used to decorate her animations could also be used for making her fraction representations more visually interesting."[13] This point captures the shift from programming code to thinking computationally in terms of such code. When Debbie was talking about making everything in her house scene a half, she had to conceive of all the halves that had to be created and consider the governing operation that would divide the number of steps that the Logo turtle would draw into half. This entailed coordinating multiple representations, including linking the numeric representation of "½," the textual representation of "one half," and a visual representation of one half of the object itself (whether it was a door, wagon, or roof). Debbie engaged with programming in designing and debugging Logo problems, but she also connected with the coding process on a computational level as "transforming" the numerical sequence to textual representation to the construction of the physical image itself.

The coding that Debbie undertook for her fraction house was an authentic learning experience for her personally, and she had the opportunity to code toward a real, in-the-world object. But equally important in terms of authenticity, Debbie's project found an enthusiastic response from her classmate Naomi. Having an audience other than a teacher is an essential feature of authentic learning environments and, in terms of schooling, represents one of the crucial affordances of Web 2.0 media.[14] The Logo-based fraction project connected mathematics and programming for students and also connected them to each other via shareable artifacts. When students programmed their instructional fraction software screens, they engaged in computational thinking and computational participation. The social interactions within Project Headlight—whether walking around the room to look at others' screens, scrolling across one another's coding scripts, or discussing potential designs with a partner—are peer interactions that were critical to the overall success of the project and precursors to the various forms of creative collaborations that are observed in today's online communities (see chapter 4). In fact, both the pedagogy of teachers (discussed in chapter 7) and the pedagogy of one's peers represent essential parts of any successful connected learning community, regardless whether they are online or offline.

The importance of these peer interactions was revealed in later apprenticeship studies that were conducted by education researcher Cynthia Carter Ching,[15] who examined teams of elementary students (some with and some without prior experience) as they designed instructional science simulation software in Logo. She found that student designers use their previous software design experiences in multiple ways and that the quality of collaborative helping interactions can shift output dramatically. Teams with experienced software designers ended up providing more collaborative assistance to their novice members, and groups of less experienced members spent far more time vying for control over the project and frequently duplicating efforts. Students who worked with experienced team members had more flexible and collaborative work arrangements in which more experienced members informally checked in with them. In contrast, students who worked with inexperienced but just slightly older students often were placed in heavily supervised activities that did few programming activities. Thus, their opportunities to develop collaborative and coding skills and grow more independent were curtailed because the range of their activities was limited. Furthermore, participation in different teams also resulted in different understandings of roles in the projects. Experienced software designers addressed a much richer set of roles, involving planning, helping, teaching, and understanding younger students' concerns and anxieties, and in the process they also engaged in computational participation.

The findings from Caperton's software design study and from Ching's apprenticeship study illustrate that treating students as designers of instructional software applications leads them to feel more invested in their own learning. Both studies also demonstrate that creating specific subject-matter content, whether a fraction house or questions for scientific inquiry, helps students learn programming significantly better than learning code in abstraction does. The analysis of the fraction design project's outcomes provided compelling evidence of the benefits for both learning fractions and learning programming, especially when compared to two other classes at the same school that had programming once a week or daily, but without the focus on creating instructional fraction software. In all these comparisons, fraction design project students improved significantly in their programming knowledge skills and their conceptual and procedural understanding of fractions.

The students' instructional software designs illustrated personal choices in representations that students created for their learners. Most important, they showcased that designing software, rather than writing code alone, provided a richer and more productive context for learning programming and mathematics. Likewise, in Ching's apprenticeship study, participating in an experienced software team raised the programming level and understanding of science for all team members. Having an experienced peer available on demand improved programming skills, affected the design of science simulations, and influenced what students learned. But to what extent does this apply to other real-world applications outside school? Caperton's research and Ching's study incorporated programming with mathematics and science, subjects that have traditionally aligned and have been associated with coding. Can programming be integrated with other academic topics and contexts as well? In this next section, we examine how this shift—from learning to program abstract code to finding real-world applications—has occurred in the development of digital stories and video game designs.

Game Design Studios and Writing Workshops in Schools

Although instructional software (like the fraction software) is grounded in school culture, whether it is purchased in the form of commercial software or designed by the students themselves, entertainment media (like videogames) often has not entered the classroom, and only recently has it become part of discussions about productive learning environments.[16] The idea of having children become game designers seemed far removed from what children could and should program. But video games are taking a prominent place in children's play, particularly boys' play. The number of hours spent in front of these screens continues to grow, as does its quality. Psychologists, sociologists, and parents are struck by a quality of engagement with video games that contrasts with children's apathy in watching television programs and doing school homework.

So the idea of extending instructional software design into game design does not seem far-fetched. In fact, it follows the same line of thinking that made instructional software into instructional software design for learning. Likewise, making games for learning instead of playing games for learning became the premise for the first study that looked at students as game programmers.[17] In a continuation of the instructional fraction design project, Yasmin Kafai asked a class of ten-year-old children to design and program their own educational fraction games. The students met every day for three months to design educational games by creating their own characters, story lines, game themes, and interactions (figure 3.2). Most of the discussion about this work has focused on the observed gender differences in the design of the games, most likely because these findings aligned well with then-popular discourse about gender differences in interest and performance in technology.[18]

Boys and girls did approach and realize their game designs differently. Most of the boys' games featured fantasy contexts with many characters and violent feedback, and the girls' games had fewer characters and no punishments for wrong answers. Most boys, for example, created adventure hunts and explorations, whereas the girls' games were divided among adventure, skill/sport, and teaching. In their choices of game themes and their programming of animation and interactions, the boys and girls offered a glimpse into what they found appealing and unappealing in the digital games and stories that they experience through other media. Making

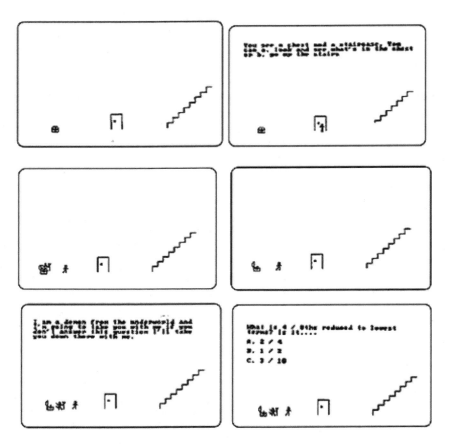

Figure 3.2
A project screen for a game design.

a game and its rules allowed the game designers to be in charge and to determine the player's place and role in a virtual world, with all the consequences. Today, programming or designing games has become one of the most popular approaches to learning programming both inside and outside schools, in a perhaps surprising alliance of promoting girls' interest and skills in programming. Many realized that boys' early interest and experience in video game play provided a major introduction to a computer culture that was slowly being discovered by women and minorities. The game design project provided visible evidence that girls could be interested in playing and making games. Although the gaming culture was initially and still is pretty much a male culture, girls and women have become a visible group of players who are prominent in casual games.[19]

Designing applications such as games appeal to an audience of avid boy and teen game players, but telling stories might relate better to an audience of girls who are avid writers and readers. Programming tools such as Alice facilitate three-dimensional story design, and Scratch promotes interactive story design with different media.[20] The game design studio offered a model for creating digital games in afterschool workshops and clubs, and a writers' workshop offered a collaborative forum and core-curricula language arts coursework to help youth learn programming as a form of composition. The widespread adoption of writing workshops at the K–12 level can be traced to the 1994 publication of writing researcher Lucy Calkins's *The Art of Teaching Writing*. The writing workshop promotes a communal setting over solitary endeavor and stresses writing as a perpetual process to generate a finished product, and it presents composition as a form of personal expression that is available to all children. This transition— from the mechanics of a skill to the social purposes of such a skill—mirrors our own interest in expanding computational thinking to computational participation.

Over most of the twentieth century, writing was a discipline in which the finished product was more important than the process by which it was created.[21] Yet Calkins's mentor, Donald Murray, cautioned educators about the craft: "Writing might be magical—but it's not magic. It's a process, a rational series of decisions and steps that every writer makes and takes, no matter what the length, the deadline, even the genre."[22] Writing, as Murray notes, does not magically appear and is not an elite skill that is limited to a select few people based on genes. It is a learned process that can be further developed through personal reflection, endeavor, and shared experience. Much like writing three decades ago, computer programming still faces this myth of the "magical."

The Scratch Writers' Workshop, designed by Quinn Burke, leverages some of the previous successes with storytelling to teach programming. The workshop considers state standards in language arts instruction and emphasizes the composition process rather than the final product or submitted deliverable. Rather than focusing on digital stories as the coded output, as previous studies did, the goal is to apply the writing workshop model to the coding process by having students compose their own digital stories through a series of designated stages. Using the workshop model pioneered by literacy researcher Lucy Calkins,[23] the Scratch Writers' Workshop had a class of middle-school students compose and code their digital stories through a series of iterations. They drafted their ideas in a writer's notebook, drew the stages of their narratives on storyboards, translated these penciled storyboards into Scratch, and used portfolios to capture their progress and share their ongoing work with peers. About 90 percent of the class completed narratives. The workshop illustrated the extent that such a structured model, as well as existing English and language arts frameworks, could be leveraged to facilitate learning programming as a form of composition.[24]

Results were promising. Over 90 percent of students completed their own digital stories using Scratch, and the narratives utilized a wide range of language arts tropes (such as static and dynamic characterization) and programming features (such as loops). A number of participants developed plotlines that were based on short graphic novellas that they had already composed in pencil and paper, giving them a better appreciation of the role played by the medium in directing a story's structure (figure 3.3). All students were novice programmers who learned basic programming concepts in the storytelling workshop. But it also became clear that writing stories favors linear structures rather than the branching conditionals that are routinely part of gaming narratives. Engaging students in programming interactive stories is one of many curricular designs that connect to already existing classroom models. It also is a possible entrance point for beginners into computational thinking and participation. We will need to expand the parameters of the Scratch Writers' Workshop to introduce a wider range of programming variables to offer further insights on the intersection of narrative and computational thinking in the classroom.

This research suggests that stories can spur children's interest in coding and that the Scratch Writers' Workshop represents a way to demystify the coding process for students and teachers by presenting it as a series of practical and interrelated steps. Such a framework underscores the connection between coding and writing as interrelated processes of composition. Digital storytelling in Scratch—particularly the workshop's focus on characterization and plot analysis—offers a new medium through which children can exercise the composition skills that they learn in traditional literacy classrooms and also be introduced to coding at an early age.

Although storytelling and coding are integral to the model and serve the same end goal, the workshop introduced them separately. Computational

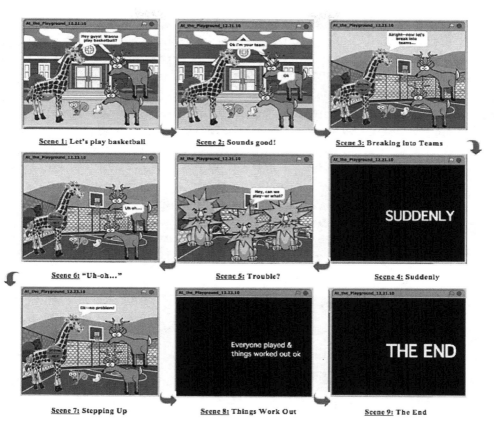

Figure 3.3
Screen shots from the Scratch Writers' Workshop project "At the Playground" by eighth-grader Andres based on his own graphic novel comic.

thinking, which emphasizes the practical and creative functionality of algorithms, offers a new way to connect coding and writing, both of which attempt to articulate a precise input to facilitate a particular output. *Make* magazine's recent partnership with the National Writing Project[25] is based on such a premise. Their workshops for literacy teachers emphasize their role as "makers" within the classroom and student writing as a tangible "product" in which the technical and creative are intertwined. Digital stories are systematically coded images and sounds that are placed in aesthetic juxtaposition, and digital stories in Scratch are likewise "products" that embody both the technical and creative elements of composition and offer a broader conception of what "writing" with computers may look like in the twenty-first century.

Moving from code to applications has been integrated with other school subjects, such as journalism, science, music, and art.[26] By leading with a particular project within a particular subject matter (whether digital stories in an English class or fraction games in a math course), programming pedagogy engages children with the potential to create real-world applications. It also builds on successful instructional practices in which educators can leverage content-based subject matter to design software that is meaningful and authentic beyond the classroom. But what about efforts that take place outside school? Helping students to write software applications, games, and stories in classrooms seems feasible. They meet every day over an extended period of time, a teacher and peers are there to answer questions, and the showcases provide a communal forum for sharing designs and highlighting accomplishments. But is it possible to do so outside the classroom, where young people do not have these guided introductions and support? Are kids motivated without a grade? What do they design? How is it different and the same? Some of the answers to these questions might be surprising: software applications for games and animations represent some of the most popular programming activities among young amateur software designers.

Designing Applications in Community Centers

Computer Clubhouses are like many other community technology centers that are located in underserved communities and provide access to computers as well as other social services. Many centers have computer labs where kids and adults can use computers for their homework, play, or work-related activities, but most of them do not offer any programming. The Intel Computer Clubhouse Network is based in community centers both in the United States and abroad, promoting creative uses of technology. The first Computer Clubhouse was started in The Computer Museum in Boston and featured the gigantic Walk-Through Computer. In 1992, Natalie Rusk, Mitchel Resnick, and Stina Cook set up an afterschool place after they observed youth sneaking back into exhibits that let visitors play and design robots. It was modeled after Seymour Papert's samba schools, providing free access but also support in form of experienced mentors and a supportive community.

The original Computer Clubhouse became so successful that more club-houses were set up in Boston and, with support from Intel Corporation, spread to other cities and countries. All the Computer Clubhouses provide youth with a variety of software, including programming software (such as Microworlds Logo), Microsoft Office, Bryce 5, Painter 7, RPG Maker™, and video, photography, and sound editing software. Although an active design culture is present in all Computer Clubhouses, programming initially was present in only few of them and was a rather marginal activity compared to the vibrant Photoshop culture.[27] Scratch was designed as a media produc-tion tool so that young people in Computer Clubhouses could program their own applications for games, digital stories, simulations, interactive art, dance videos, or other genres of work that they already loved to do.

How and why youth moved from being users of software packages to being Scratch designers of digital media applications illustrates program-ming's motivational appeal. When the first version of Scratch was intro-duced in a Computer Clubhouse in Los Angeles and loaded on several of the computers in fall 2004, few members created anything using the new software. But in winter 2005, a steady stream of undergraduate men-tors joined the Clubhouse to help and learn programming themselves. A striking rise in Scratch activities occurred as youth members encouraged each other to try the program, and mentors worked with youth to create their first Scratch projects. Mentors often engaged youth who had never worked in Scratch before by asking them to import some of the hundreds of screenshots and graphics files that they had stored in their folders on the Clubhouse server. At that point, youth projects on the server represented mostly graphics-only projects. But within a few months of the introduction of Scratch, printouts of Scratch screen designs began to cover the walls of the Clubhouse, and it became the leading design activity.

By winter 2006, interest in Scratch had grown, and new things were hap-pening within the Clubhouse culture. Scratch became a measure of mem-bership in the local Clubhouse culture, and creating and storing Scratch projects on the central server for others to play moved the previously rare and isolated programming activity into a communal affair. Also, groups of youth began working collaboratively together to create projects, and they created flashy team names, such as "DGMM," for the "Dang Good Money Makers." Education researcher Kylie Peppler observed how young people began to work independently of mentoring support on the complex projects and problems that they encountered in Scratch. Youth were seen mentoring other youth in Scratch, and some emerged as general experts that mentors, coordinators, and other youth consulted for help. Others specialized in certain genres or tricks within Scratch, and they too were called on by their peers and mentors.[28]

A compelling example of videogame design is "Metal Slug Hell Zone X." It was created by a fifteen-year-old Latino designer named Jorge, who modeled the piece after a popular videogame with a similar title.[29] The original *Metal Slug* game is a futuristic "run and gun videogame" that is known for its humor, fluid hand-drawn animation, and fast-paced, two-player action. Jorge brought his passion and experience in video gaming to the Clubhouse, where he spent most of his time working on Scratch projects that involved recreations of video games. "Metal Slug Hell Zone X" was his second project, and it incorporated many well-known features from the original video game but also added new and unexpected features. The start of the video game was fairly traditional. A title screen listed four avatars that players could choose by pressing a button. The game began with a barren purple desert landscape and moving clouds. Players could use arrow keys to have their selected avatar move forward or backward, crouch, jump, and fire a gun. As shown by the opening sequence, avatar choices, background scrolling, and action items, Jorge used his prior knowledge of the Metal Slug games and interests in video gaming to forge connections to Scratch while making his video game.

"Metal Slug Hell Zone X" took several months to design, and it incorporated complex technical features that could be considered illustrative of computational thinking. Jorge discovered how to create a side-scrolling game and complicated types of animation by using difficult programming concepts, including variables, loops, conditional statements, communication and synchronization commands (such as broadcast and when-receive), and Boolean logic. Designing the game motivated Jorge's engagement with programming. He learned how to design for interactive play and redesigned his program several times, discovering that it can be friendlier to the user to design a game that responds to standard key strokes (such as right and left arrow keys) rather than random characters on the keyboard. In addition, he used a full suite of creative software and not just programming software. Using the Scratch Paint Editor (an image editor), Jorge realistically animated the avatar as it moved. He made sketches based on playing the original video game, downloaded sample avatars from Internet fan sites, and refined each frame of the movement in the Paint Editor for smooth stop-action animation. With the visual programming capabilities of Scratch, Jorge animated these images to respond to keystrokes so that the avatar walks effortlessly across the screen or jumps when prompted by control keys.

These shifts from creating visual designs to programming animations illustrate Jorge's pathway into computational thinking. This shifted toward computational participation as Jorge tweaked his game to become more user-accessible and more closely resemble the online culture specific to designing and making fan videogames. Jorge used standard design conventions found in videogames and created special responses for when the avatar is told to do something (such as shoot) while crouching or jumping. Using Scratch helped Jorge understand how games are made by professional production specialists, and he also networked with other fans of the original game, who, like himself, wanted to play and create amateur spin-off productions as part of the do-it-yourself culture.

Just like Debbie's instructional fraction software, Jorge's "Metal Slug Hell Zone X" game software illustrated personal connections to artistic and technical domains. It also illustrated the importance of social connections in the days before Web 2.0. For Debbie, these were located with her classmates and the third-graders of Project Headlight, and for Jorge, they were located with the local Computer Clubhouse community (which provided an appreciative and supportive audience) and with online fan player and gaming communities. Unlike Debbie's software, which was part of a classroom project, Jorge's design of the video game was self-initiated by Jorge. He remade a game that he enjoyed playing and then added his own interpretations, not straying too far from the original while still adding his own twists. It is not unusual for players to design their own games. In fact, many Project Headlight students confessed that they would prefer to program a fraction game than fraction software.

Today character and level editors are available with many games, allowing players to add new features and thus extend the playability of games, but in the 1980s and 1990s, when game companies kept close tabs on the content and design of video games, these features were virtually unheard of. These amateur efforts all share the spirit of self-produced and originated projects.[30] Most DIY efforts take place within the context of informal, lunchtime computer clubs rather than traditional classrooms, and DIY efforts are equally prominent in writing and publishing. Studies of fan fiction sites and of young people's use of zines point to ways that youth are enjoying academic styles of writing, publishing, and critiquing in the out-of-school hours, and developing identities as writers in the process. Designing games and writing stories, in and out of schools, showcase how designing software applications can become a rich way of participating as producers and not just as consumers in the digital culture.

Software Application Design Becomes Popular

Today, design courses for applications ("apps")[31] are increasingly popular and ought to be encouraged to broaden participation. By widening the walls,[32] programming can be applied to a range of design activities rather than just narrow technical ones. As eighth-grader Daryl noted after he completed his own digital story in the Scratch Writers' Workshop, "Scratch can do almost anything. It has hundreds of controls, hundreds of images, and you can even take ones off the Internet.... And so all you need to do is have a focus."[33] Designing specific applications—whether video games or digital stories—represents such a focus, particularly when the applications are further grounded by personally and socially authentic learning contexts, such as game-making studios and writing workshops.

Designing applications also can be considered a direct and accessible application of Jeannette Wing's computational thinking. It captures key aspects of designing systems, solving problems, and understanding human behaviors because designing an application like a game or simulation involves the creation of a system that requires designers to think about how users will interface with the applications they design and how features can be implemented according to their intentions. On a personal level, designing applications has generated broad interest and a high success rate in getting youth interested in computer programming. Perhaps this is why making games for learning has interested many for-profit and nonprofit groups.

Nowhere is this more evident than in the proliferation of video game-making competitions such as Globaloria's Globey Awards, Advanced Micro Devices' AMD Changing the Game contest, the Games for Change Awards, as well as the National STEM Video Game Design Challenge (cosponsored by the White House). These competitions instill a sense of empowerment, both personal and social, that participants can make what they use, and this empowerment is characteristic of the self-reliance and drive of the wider DIY movement since the advent of Web. 2.0. They all point toward the relevance of communities where ideas and designs can be created and commented on, shared with others, and even remixed. The social contexts and cultural practices are the focus of the next chapters.

4   From Tools to Communities

The Scratch online site opened in May 2007 with little fanfare. Yet a few well-placed tech reviews, particularly a May 14 article in BBC *News online—was enough to generate a surge of enthusiastic traffic that shut down the Scratch site temporarily. Soon new visitors were making Scratch online their own by creating individual profiles, sharing comments, and uploading their own programs in Scratch code. Then in June 2008 something new occurred at the site. Three members of the Scratch online community founded Green Bear Productions and opened an account online to create high-quality video games collaboratively. The founders—ages eight, thirteen, and fifteen—soon created a video game entitled "Pearl Harbor" that functioned like a digital version of the classic* Battleship. *The sophistication of the game's graphics and the ease of game play attracted hundreds of views and downloads on its initial release. Multiple remixes of the project soon followed. As Green Bear Productions explains at its website, "we had a lot of people who wanted to join us," and membership within the group jumped to eighteen. Soon Green Bear Productions created games such as "Forest Frenzy" and "A Night at Dreary Castle" that reflected the designers' growing sophistication in creating graphics, plotlines, and game play. "Forest Frenzy" had nineteen versions over a period of multiple months before a final glitch-free version was completed.[1]*

In the collaborative and social climate of Web 2.0,[2] online creative collaborative production like that of Green Bear Productions is not unheard of, but at Green Bear Productions, it is young people, not adults, who organized this collaborative effort, and most had never met each other in person before. Other than two of the founding members, none of Green Bear's members had ever personally met the others in the group. Members of the company were located in different places, even different time zones, and came together based on their common interest in collaborating on Scratch projects. And perhaps more surprising, the group's members came together to design and program their own video games. Programming, once largely perceived as an individual (even asocial) activity, was unexpectedly becoming a communal affair on the Scratch site.

Seymour Papert always considered learning to be a communal practice and cited his experiences with Brazil's samba schools as a model for a more natural and socialized experience to learn any technical skill.[3] For Papert, learning the technique of the complicated samba was not simply a matter of skill-and-drill memorization but was linked to the experience of socializing in dance halls. As children, adults, and the elderly gathered in the hall, they celebrated a cultural pastime in which the central ritual is absorbed from a young age. The dance steps and subtle movements and gestures are part of the wider social fabric of the scene.

South American dance halls on warm weekend evenings may appear to be the opposite climate of the decidedly more austere environment of U.S. computer labs. But this was precisely the point as Papert wished to draw attention to just how asocial such computer labs were. He challenged educators to make learning with computers a more social, even communal experience. To this day, this is still not the case. Computing—as it typically is done in schools—appears to be an asocial activity in which children operate at their own machines. Getting up from one's machine is a breach of conduct within schools, and looking at another's screen borders on cheating.

This rigidly individualistic approach that is characteristic of schools is unlike the approach that is used in the software industry itself, in which developers generally spend 30 percent of their time working alone, 50 percent working with one other person, and 20 percent working with two or more people.[4] A walk around one of Google's or Apple's development offices reveals the social nature of software development: hallways are expansive, doorways are wide and free of doors, and walls are glass. Rather than stifling interaction, the architectural design of such spaces encourages it.[5]

The point of teaching young people to use introductory programming languages is not to help them become computer scientists or secure a spot at Google or Apple but rather to help them become more effective creators and discerning consumers of digital media. To do this, we need to understand how coding has shifted into a collaborative and social activity among some young users and what the implications of this social turn are in terms of the future of children's learning in and out of schools. The first part of the chapter examines this shift away from programming tools and toward programming communities and the ways that making coding accessible has inspired youth communities that code collaboratively. The second part of the chapter examines two such online collaborations from the Scratch website, exploring their origins and projects. The final part of the chapter explores ways that these types of collaborations can be furthered both in and out of schools. Can environments for such peer-supported collaborative learning be engineered, and what evidence do we have of successes and failures in this area?

Making Coding More Accessible: The Rise of the Tool

Over the past twenty years, most efforts to facilitate teaching and learning programming have focused less on facilitating collaboration and more on designing more intuitive and supportive programming tools. When Papert introduced Logo as a tool to make programming more intuitive and sociable for children, he unwittingly launched a veritable cottage industry of introductory programming languages based on his model. Nearly two hundred different variations of Logo have emerged so far with more still in development—including variants like Cricket Logo (which applies the Logo language to programmable hand-held robotic toys), Terrapin Logo (which allows the inclusion of multivoice music), and Logo3D (which adds an entirely new dimension to the original two-dimensional output).[6]

Other introductory programming languages shared Logo's goal to make programming more accessible and intuitive to young users. This included computer pioneer Alan Kay's Smalltalk and later developments Squeak and eToys, whose programming environment allowed users to create programs and also examine and modify the tool itself.[7] Science educator Andrea diSessa's Boxer programming language built on the Logo model but introduced clickable "boxes" as the site of programming commands, shifting code from a series of typed lines to a number of juxtaposed and interrelated coded boxes.[8] Computer scientist Mark Guzdial promoted embedded graphical scaffolds in Emile, a programming environment that helped beginners to grasp coding concepts via a concrete, step-by-step approach. Such hands-on graphical illustration is often necessary for beginning programmers, Guzdial points out, because they need tools that make code less cumbersome in terms of syntax, more responsive in terms of output, and more personally relevant in terms of end products.[9]

The element of personal relevance is crucial. As the previous chapter points out, when children are drawn to particular applications—whether a video game, digital story, or musical animation—programming becomes more compelling as a tool for personal expression. Media education researchers Sarah Holloway and Gill Valentine's examination of children's usage of digital media concludes that, contrary to the prevailing sentiment, technologies are not intrinsic motivators but become "cool tools" that drive learning only when they directly relate to the social context of children's everyday online and offline lives.[10]

This same point is supported by computer scientists Caitlin Kelleher and Randy Pausch's extensive taxonomy of dozens of introductory programming environments. They find that although improved technology has made the underlying mechanics of computer science more manageable for young users, the entrenched social and cultural stigmas surrounding programming can stifle such motivation. These barriers are expressed in stereotypes such as "programming is for nerds," "programming is isolating," and "only boys like programming," which for Kelleher and Pausch represent the real challenge of getting more children interested in computer programming. Software designers can repeatedly address and smooth over the most persistent technical issues, but engaging children with code can be nearly impossible after they make up their minds that it is simply not for them.[11]

As educational researcher Jane Margolis and her colleagues have demonstrated, these social stigmas are adopted by children, school counselors, and teachers and appear as early as elementary school. With these social and cultural stigmas reinforced throughout a child's K–12 education, it is unsurprising that even when children have the opportunity to attend college, few have the confidence, interest, and skill sets to pursue studies in computer science or engineering in general.[12]

Putting programming tools into children's hands at earlier ages is an imperative. Reflecting on the growing number of introductory programming tools that are available to children, Scratch designers Mitchel Resnick and Brian Silverman outlined three essential principles that designers need to be mindful of when designing computational construction kits like Logo and its brood.[13] Employing the metaphor of a house, Resnick and Silverman posited that if a tool is to be adopted by young users, it needs to address the following three aspects:

• *Low floors*: The tool must be intuitive enough to allow new users to acclimate to it gradually and with a degree of confidence.

• *High ceilings*: The tool must allow experienced users to create increasingly complex applications that grow more intricate and nuanced as their proficiency in using the tool increases.

• *Wide walls*: The tool must allow for a wide range of projects, let users tap into elements of personal experience and popular culture, and let them design and develop programs that are unique and represent their own interests and backgrounds.

These three components—low floors, high ceilings, and wide walls—have been adopted by the leading educational programming tools such as university-designed Agentsheets, Alice, Gamestar Mechanic, Scratch, and StarLogo as well as commercially developed tools such as Kodu.[14] But despite the importance of these three elements, the real shift is the opening of new communities, or *windows* (if we continue with a fourth element of the house metaphor), to facilitate creating digital media. The creation of digital communities represents the new frontier in terms of making computer programming a more accessible skill for youth. Where and how do children look to share the applications that they create? And perhaps even more important, where and how do they look to learn to make applications?

Community has always been tacitly recognized as one of the key aspects for learning any skill set, from fundamental skills (like learning how to speak) to specialized skills (like creating programmable media). Educators have used notions of "communities of practice"[15] as well as "affinity groups" and "affinity spaces"[16] to try to understand the role that is played by social interplay in the learning process. This focus on community relates directly to the rise of the Internet as a new way to interact with others. As the Web has evolved, society's comprehension of what is meant by the notion of community has shifted tremendously in a very short amount of time. Chatrooms, massive multiplayer online role-playing games, and social networks (such as Facebook, Twitter, and LinkedIn) are examples of communities that are virtual but have roots in the physical presence of daily life. The capacity to build is another characteristic of Web 2.0 technology. Works by legal scholar Yochai Benkler and media researcher Clay

Shirky optimistically herald such building as an unprecedented civic and financial opportunity for global communities to develop around mutual interests and common causes.[17]

Despite cognitive research on the importance of community for learning, as well as the spike in online communities that is characteristic of Web 2.0 and the wider do-it-yourself movement, the idea of programming communities is still relatively new. Some early work that looked at how children learn to code examined the challenges and opportunities of having students work together in small teams.[18] But programming in K–12 contexts is still almost always taught as an individual activity (as are most subjects in school). Perhaps the most successful collaborative design in teaching children how to code has been the introduction of pair programming activities over the past decade. Sitting side by side at the same computer, one child takes the role of the "driver" who inputs the code, and the other plays the "navigator" who reviews each inputted line, checking its syntax and compatibility with previous inputs. These roles switch periodically. Within the industry itself, pair programming has demonstrated increased accuracy in coded scripts and more reliable output.[19] Among children, this has also been the case, but with young programmers, studies have demonstrated that children's motivation to program and persist at troubleshooting their own code increases significantly when they work in pairs.[20] This important third element suggests that pair programming establishes a modicum of checks and balances for coding and also helps develop a more communal atmosphere for learning.

This communal atmosphere for programming first migrated online with the development of MOOSE Crossing in 1997.[21] Based on computer scientist Amy Bruckman's design and research, MOOSE Crossing was purely a text-based platform (which is characteristic of the massive role playing or multiuser dungeons of the time period). Set within a virtual castle, students explored their environment through words alone. Despite the lack of the graphics and animations that characterize today's online worlds, MOOSE Crossing was unique at that time. It was the first online educational platform to engage young users by allowing them to interact with their peers online and to add to the virtual domain by programming their own characters, animals, and rooms within the castle—each of which had programmable parameters. Within MOOSE Crossing, children learned programming within a networked community. Young programmers had the opportunity to view others' coded scripts and ask each other for support as they designed their own programmable objects. Whereas Resnick and Silverman focused on principles for creating effective tools for learning programming, Bruckman focused on principles for creating meaningful online communities for learning programming at earlier ages:

• Maximize each individual's opportunities for creative expression and active participation.

• Assume that average people are smarter and more creative than what is typically assumed.

• Encourage users to be creators of content, and maintain quality by enforcing a minimal set of community standards.

• Develop an infrastructure for community support for learning.[22]

These four points are not the only guidelines for designing meaningful online spaces for learning programming, and they represent design principles that apply to many scenarios, not just creating spaces to learn programming online. But in 1997, when Bruckman completed her research, they represented what was then the clearest articulation of how to develop what we refer to as the new windows for learning programming. They also articulate the underlying principles that led to the development of the online Scratch community.[23]

Going Social: The Tool *Is* the Community

When I think about it, recognition for my work is what really drew me into Scratch. Other things played a part, but the feeling that my work would be seen is what really motivated me.

—Fourteen-year-old member of Scratch Community, screen-name "Hobbit"[24]

The motto at the Scratch website (http://scratch.mit.edu) reads "Imagine, Program, Share," although the unofficial motto for many members (such as "Hobbit") may very well be "See and be seen." One primary attraction for youth in creating applications rather than simply generating code has always been sharing such applications with others and gaining status with these shared creations (see chapter 3). Even before the launch of the Scratch website, early use of the Scratch tool in its beta stages at a Computer Clubhouse revealed that the aspiring programmers wanted to show off what they had created. Two years of testing the tool with youth members and mentors resulted in a vibrant design community within the Clubhouse that developed hundreds of different games.[25]

These hundreds of games from local offline community centers quickly grew into thousands, tens of thousands, and now millions. Dubbed "the YouTube of interactive media," the Scratch website currently has 1.5 million registered members (referred to as "Scratchers"), and they have uploaded over 3 million projects since its launch in 2007. Scratchers range in age from five to seventy, but most members fall between the ages of eleven and twenty-one. The mean age of Scratchers is fifteen. Scratch has visitors from nearly seventeen thousand cities worldwide, and its programmable bricks are translated into over forty languages.[26] Although many websites (such as YouTube and Flickr) support uploading and downloading user-generated content, the Scratch website offers a platform for users to share their own programmed interactive media.[27] Uploading and downloading projects on the site is an exchange of information, but it also is an exchange of personally crafted content that can be downloaded and remixed by others to build entirely new projects. As users grow familiar with the Scratch site, they encounter a variety of projects and coding scripts that they can sample and remix.

When Scratch team member Andrés Monroy-Hernández set out to create the first online community for Scratch, Bruckman's MOOSE Crossing and her recommendations for youth communities of programmers served as a model. But both Bruckman and Monroy-Hernández were inspired by Papert's constructionist principles. He wanted Scratch to become "a sort of 'Samba school' where novices and experts would gather to read, write, and remix Scratch literature. I wanted to take Scratch from being 'just' a good tool to a space where peers gather to create, share, remix, and even just 'hang out': a commons-based peer production community. This meant giving people access to an audience, potential collaborators, and a repository of inspirational creations that creators could learn and remix from."[28]

The remarkable success of the online Scratch community signals this shift from a programming tool to a community of programmers. Other introductory programming tools are following Scratch's lead. The programming language Alice team, for example, is developing the Looking Glass Community as an online extension of its game tool.[29] The for-profit commercial developments of Microsoft's Kodu and Recreational Design

Software's Game-Maker tools have developed online communities since 2012. Papert's assessment of the Logo turtle as an "object-to-think-with" may now be replaced with these programmable and shareable applications as "objects-to-share-with."[30] To make is to connect,[31] and these programmable applications are devices that have real currency and relevance in society's growing migration toward online participation and partnerships, as research by Mizuko Ito and colleagues (2009) showed. Those who are good at making things are increasingly also those who are good at sharing things. As this trend from tools to communities suggests, to make is to share, and to share is to make.

What does this collaborative sharing and making of computer programs look like? How does the Scratch website open up new windows for developing communities of youth programming? As suggested by community member Hobbit at the outset of this section, reception plays a prominent role. When a browser is opened to the website, this element of "see and be seen" becomes readily apparent (figure 4.1). This main page (termed "the front page" by community members) features the most popular and timely projects, which are organized in galleries such as "Featured Projects," "Top Viewed," and "Featured Studios," and the galleries of individual community members, who apply to the Scratch team to "curate" their own assortment of Scratch projects. The page changes daily, and to "make front page" is a major source of status and pride among Scratchers—particularly among the most dedicated members.

Scratch team member Karen Brennan's extensive interviews with various members of the online community reveal the importance of finding an online audience and the exposure offered by the front page. According to "Sonia," age sixteen, "What makes the online community good is … being able to comment on other people's projects. Because getting feedback on something you made is a lot better than just making it and not having anyone see it. So, it kind of gives a purpose to making it."[32] Another Scratcher, "Jenson," age eleven, also states that audience reception is crucial: "In my opinion, every programmer probably has a hope that somebody's going to view it."[33]

Attracting viewers at the Scratch website is not simply a matter of achieving front-page status, however. Through project views and clickable "Love-Its," Scratch users can monitor numbers and assess popularity. More important, every project posted at the Scratch website has a "Comments"

Figure 4.1
Galleries of projects from the Scratch home page.

section where other community members can share their thoughts. Comments can include questions, advice, criticism (Scratch team members regularly vet for "constructive criticism"), and praise (such as "Love it!" and "Cool project!"). Scratch team members recently have focused on using basic encouragement and attribution via the Comments feature to welcome new users to the site and encourage them to explore projects online with the personal connections that are possible through the Comments section.[34] Even the simplest of lines offering positive feedback can spur users forward with their own programming.

The Forums section on the website provides a platform for sharing, questioning, or commenting on all things Scratch. How to get a project on the front page is a popular topic in the Forums section, but members also post to find and "friend" other potential collaborators, brainstorm project ideas, and request and share technical know-how (such as how to create more advanced scrolling games or how to import video into Scratch as an animation). The sharing that takes place in the Forums (particularly that related to technical expertise) has now led to the development of a Scratch-related wiki that includes nearly a thousand unique pages, most of which have been created not by the MIT Scratch team but by Scratchers themselves.[35]

Although there used to be a distinction between the Scratch software as the programming tool and the online website as the corresponding community, the tremendous growth of this community and its resources demonstrates its utility as a tool itself. In the new version of Scratch 2.0, the Scratch design team no longer makes any division between Scratch as a tool and Scratch as a community. Young designers code and communicate at a single website. The expectation is that these new windows of community will ultimately make it easier for people to connect and collaborate, thus further dropping the floors, raising the ceilings, and widening the walls for everyone. The community case studies that follow exemplify these three elements.

Youth DIY Creative Collaborations: Game Companies, Coloring Contests, and Book Clubs

Green Bear Productions, the fledgling company mentioned at the beginning of this chapter, provides a vivid illustration of the do-it-yourself collaborative spirit of the Scratch community. For Green Bear, effective collaboration was not achieved by developing previously existing interpersonal ties because out of the team's eighteen members, only the two founders knew each other beforehand. Their connection was made by leveraging the power of common interests and a shared tool. To become a member of Green Bear Productions, Scratch users "applied" to the company. This usually meant that they sent the founding members an online message expressing interest and offered an URL to their previous work at the Scratch website to demonstrate their prowess in using graphics, plotting a storyline, or developing coding scripts for gameplay (figure 4.2).

If accepted, Scratchers became full members of a democracy and could volunteer game ideas, which the rest of the production team voted on before reaching a final decision. After a project was selected, the team assigned roles and arranged a production schedule. The founders encouraged users to follow a game to its completion before starting any additional projects. All of Green Bear's games entailed alpha and multiple beta versions before a final, glitch-free version was produced and released on the website.

Green Bear Productions Company was the one of the first teams to call itself a production company within Scratch, embodying the open-source community spirit with very young users. Computer scientists Kurt Luther and Amy Bruckman, who have studied online creative communities that make interactive digital media, note that when collaborations succeed, they produce content that supersede what any single member could have accomplished on their own.[36] The problem, they point out, is that these collaborations disband more often than they succeed. This makes the success of Green Bear Productions even more surprising, especially because young people and not adults drove this enterprise.

Figure 4.2
A selection of Green Bear Production games: "Pearl Harbor," "Retro Claw Capture," and "Night at the Dreary Castle." http://scratch.mit.edu/galleries/view/21935.

What makes kids join Scratch and form companies like Green Bear Productions? This was what researcher Karen Brennan of the Scratch team intended to uncover as part of her doctoral dissertation at MIT. After interviewing several members who had formed and joined such companies, she discovered that altruism was not necessarily the members' primary motivation. Scratcher "Lana," seventeen years old, explains:

It's not really a thing that people are doing out of goodwill—it's out of interest. It's always good when you have that enthusiasm because that's the only thing that keeps it going. You have to communicate. People in your collaborations should know exactly what to expect and what they want to of this. Because if their expectations aren't met and you're kind of forcing your own views on them and you aren't paying attention to their opinion, they'll probably get bored with the project. For that reason, it's always good to come to an agreement before you make a project. I think that's the main thing.[37]

Yet other members of Scratch companies, such as ten-year-old "Chelsey," indicate that increased and more sophisticated output is not the primary driver. Responding to a question about what was the "greatest thing" about starting and working within a Scratch company, she explains:

Greatest things? I've met—I've made loads of new friends. It's really fun just making projects together rather than doing them on my own.[38]

One study examined the nature of Green Bear members' online exchanges as they developed their projects through the galleries on the Scratch website. After analyzing three months of chat-based textual exchanges (approximately 1,470 lines), the study found that the team's online exchanges were context-related (such as scheduling or technology specifications) 32 percent of the time, task-related to the project 19 percent of the time, and socioemotional (socializing by joking or relating feelings) 49 percent of the time.[39] This research suggests that socializing is a primary driver behind such online collaboration—even in collaborations that are formal enough to refer to themselves as companies.

If all collaborations in the Scratch community had been about kids making games, it might have become a typical "geek club." Constructing projects in such a methodical manner requires people who are able to identify the composite parts of a project, delegate duties, ensure that they are completed in a timely manner, and—perhaps most difficult—reassemble the composite parts to form a unified whole. This approach is characteristic of very high ceilings—using modularization to break down the programming task into a series of independent systems.[40] But the Scratch community, like the Scratch programming language, provides wide walls as well, and the socialization that played a significant role in Green Bear Productions plays an even more prominent role in some of the most common collaborations at the website.

Large Scratch collaborations among four or more members usually occur through digital "chain letter" projects in which an individual user creates a project that prompts other users to contribute to its content.[41] Examples of these digital chain letter projects are "Add yourself to the group photo" in which other users are invited to share a picture of themselves or their avatars to the Scratch stage (figure 4.3). Others include "Add yourself to the race," "Add yourself as a baby," and "Add yourself as the Scratch Cat."

What these chain letter projects lack in complex coding, they make up for popularity, often attracting thousands of contributors, which helps users—particularly new users—to establish a sense of community at the website. Contributing to these low-threshold projects is pressure-free and playfully social rather than one that is focused on a particular end goal. Young users can contribute to a project with hundreds of others in a low-pressure environment.

This ability to "add and pass on" also serves as the basis for one of the most interesting forms of online collaborations at the website—role-playing games (RPGs)—in which users use the galleries section to spin storylines of assorted characters and plot twists.[42] Most of these RPG storylines are serialized through the comments section underneath a project, and the project serves as a place to add visuals (like characters and settings) that are based on the developments in the RPG. Currently, more than five

Figure 4.3
A selection of the popular Scratch "Add yourself" chain projects: "Add yourself to the race," "Add yourself as a baby," and "Add yourself as the Scratch Cat."

thousand Scratch galleries have *RPG* in their titles or descriptions with group sizes ranging from a few members to a thousand players. The largest RPG included over 600,000 comments, nearly two thousand projects, and about a thousand players.

Some popular RPGs at the Scratch website are fan-based and draw on the characters and storylines from books and movies (like the Harry Potter books and films) and television shows (such as *Twilight*). Popular fiction (like the Warriors series of young adult novels) is another source. The Warriors novels follow the adventures of four cat clans who live in the forest and deal with issues of loyalty and friendship. One RPG, Warriors of the Blue (WOB), includes roughly 250 members, 80 percent of whom are girls. Like Green Bear Productions, WOB encourages members to participate but is maintained by a central moderator (screen name "MidnightBlaze") who sets the rules for stimulating plot development. The WOB gallery includes a long description of the Warriors' world that was written by MidnightBlaze and describes the rules for participating in the group. As with Green Bear Productions, people need to ask permission to join WOB, which is granted by WOB creator MidnightBlaze and a few other longstanding members. Likewise, in role playing, MidnightBlaze assumes a more prominent role as the collab's creator. She guards the stories by providing prophecies (a central element of the Warriors novels), correcting members if they get an element wrong, and supporting a culture where members ask for her permission before they move forward with new ideas. In fact, members curry her attention, showing delight when she replies to comments or subplots and frustration when she ignores them. MidnightBlaze's leadership is thus enacted through her own actions and through the interactions of others who reinforce her position (even in her absence) and who extend her authority by policing on her behalf.

Like the add-on chain letter projects, WOB's development of storylines in the Comments feature is another low barrier for participation. But there are additional and more explicit rules as well. The site owner, MidnightBlaze, vets all storylines and removes comments that do not adhere to the narrative of the Warriors novels. In addition, she and other longstanding members supplement the narrative by programming characterizations, basic animations, and background music on the Scratch screen based on the comments-based storyline (figure 4.4). Thus, the most popular characters and storylines are, in a sense, identified and rewarded by MidnightBlaze

Figure 4.4
A selection of Warriors of the Blue projects featuring cat characters, sometimes with
wings and special powers.

and her senior team when they opt to program these individual aspects of
the overall story arc.

The observations of these three different DIY collaborations in Scratch
are compelling and, much like gaming communities, provide examples of
self-organized learning and design communities. With the RPG community
Warriors of the Blue, only a few of the senior members do coding, whereas
the chain letters required little programming by any member. The remaining members focus their contributions to the comments section, which are
then vetted by these senior members. Although not all members program
at the collab, the RPG acts as a community of practice, bringing in new
members who grow to understand the prevailing rules of the group. Those
who remain and contribute regularly using the designated comments section eventually have the opportunity to ascend to a more senior position
and begin coding the animations and music to accompany the ongoing
script. A pathway, however informal, is in place.

This element of a pathway is key. Five elements appear to be crucial
to the success of online collaborations around open-source software projects, whether animated movies, interactive video games, or some hybrid
between the two.[43] Successful collaborations seem to have members who
are intrinsically motivated and self-selected for tasks, a charismatic and
capable leader, a meritocratic and rational culture, a modular and granular
division of labor, and collaborative technologies. Green Bear Productions
and Warriors of the Blue both incorporate these elements. Although WOB
was run more as a top-down hierarchy than the more democratic Green
Bear, both collabs had founders who hosted the rest of the team at their
site and who were the main enforcers of the group's rules. Likewise, both

groups utilized the technical elements of the Scratch website to delineate individual contributions. For Green Bear, multiple iterations of projects were posted at the galleries section. For WOB, participants used the comments feature in innovative (and unexpected) ways to serialize narratives by individual contributions.

The pathway that these two collabs were able to chart on their own is not one that most Scratch members are able to follow as a viable pathway. The high level of collaboration that these two collabs illustrate represents the exception rather than the norm at the Scratch website. A recent analysis of five thousand randomly sampled Scratch user profiles online reveals that less than half had ever submitted any project online, remixed another's work, or collaborated with others on a single project.[44] This is typical of most online sites and is not surprising. Despite the myth that today's children are all eager "digital natives," recent research suggests that children are less empowered and galvanized by digital media than some might think.[45]

An exploratory study of middle-school students who were using an early version of the Scratch website showed that many children are uncomfortable with sharing their projects online, are nervous about the comments they will receive, and want to post the project only when it is "just right."[46] Even after users submit their work, there is no assurance that they will find the audience and attention that motivate many to share online. Max O. Lorenz's 80/20 distribution curve[47] (20 percent of a population receives 80 percent of the attention) plays out in Scratch. An examination of 2.2 million projects at the Scratch site showed that the 20 percent most-viewed Scratchers received 95.6 percent of views, and the other 80 percent of Scratchers received 4.4 percent of views.[48] Recognizing these steep discrepancies in collaboration and participation, the Scratch team began to conceive of ways to bring together more of its users online.

Initiating DIY Youth Collaborations: Creating Online Collabs and Camps in Schools

In 2010, a new Scratch research focus on collaboration and computation in a networked commons looked at how learning to program and learning to participate could be mutually beneficial. Would a forum help new users grow more comfortable sharing their own work online and find others with like interests? Could more experienced users serve as mentors to these new users? To this end, the first annual Collab Challenge was launched at the Scratch website in January 2011, and Collab Camps were held in July 2011 and January 2012 (figure 4.5).[49]

Open to the entire community, the first Collab Challenge ran from January to early March 2011. Each team needed to have a minimum of two participants; integrate three unique, preselected images into its projects; upload an initial draft midway through the competition to receive

Scratch Collab Challenge

What can you and other Scratchers create together using three images and a lot of imagination? We've created the Scratch Collab Challenge to find out.

1. **Register** your group or collab here as soon as possible.

2. **Make a project** with your collab that uses these three images. Be creative in using the sprites.

COLLAB CAMP
MUSIC MASHUPS

February 8, 2012 – March 31, 2012

Collab Camp is a virtual event in the Scratch online community where Scratch members form collabs, or groups, and create Scratch projects together. This camp's theme is music mashups.

Figure 4.5
The initial announcement for the Collab Challenge and two Collab Camps, which centered on interactive stories and musical video mash-ups.

constructive feedback from the Scratch team; and submit a final project three weeks later. The draft and final projects were exhibited in a Collab gallery where participants could view and comment on each other's projects. Teams that integrated three disparate images using their own original ideas and coding sequences had their projects featured on the Scratch homepage, which is a desirable status for many in the community.

A total of fifty-two collab teams (139 participants) registered to participate in the initial Collab Challenge in January 2011. About 41.7 percent of the participants were relative newcomers to the community, and 48 percent of the participants had been on Scratch for more than three months.[50] Comments made by experienced Scratchers suggest that the Challenge stimulated renewed interest in participating in the online community. One Scratcher who had been with the community for over two years thanked the team for hosting the Challenge:

I want to personally thank all of you for throwing the Collab Challenge. Taking the time to create this has allowed me to work with some of the best scratchers—something that I think we all appreciate. I hope that you continue to do more challenges like this one in the future.[51]

Fifty-two of the groups that registered for the Collab Challenge in January submitted a first draft of a project by mid-February, and twenty-six submitted a final version by the end of March. Although K. Luther and colleagues found that only 13 percent of collabs on the digital media site Newgrounds succeeded in completing a finished project,[52] a full 50 percent of the Scratch collabs that submitted an initial version of a project to the Collab Challenge succeeded in submitting a final version. Although these numbers reflect a small number of reference points, they suggest the potential for success of a lightly structured Challenge environment in which participants receive constructive feedback on drafts and have preestablished deadlines to help define and tier goals.

This element of "light structure" suggests that schools can help children engage in the computational participation that characterizes these online collaborations. After a class of high school freshmen participated in the first Scratch Collab Challenge, Yasmin Kafai and her research team paired their analysis of online collaboration at the website with offline observations and interviews with the students themselves as they worked in teams of four to eight students for course credit. Initially, the high school students were intrigued by the challenge for the sake of the same "see and be seen" mentality that draws many to the website. "I like participating in the [Collab] project because I got to contribute to the cool projects on the website," said one student. Another praised the "safe" nature of sharing projects online in the constructive confines of the Scratch Collab gallery because the structure of the Challenge was an improvement on the "anything goes" feedback that often accompanies peer-to-peer feedback in less moderated forums:[53] "It is always really helpful to have positive feedback instead of continual accusations like 'Make this better' or 'Just do it,'" the participant noted in the postclass interview.[54]

What was especially heartening was that the high school students who participated the online Collab Challenge became aware of the Scratch online community as a place to gain and leverage an audience. One group that created a brickbreaker video game for the Challenge, for example, researched various types of its own game on the Scratch site and built its game to improve on the existing versions at the site. Another group ignored feedback from classroom teachers about making their projects more intuitive but responded to online comments about developing a better interface by adding project notes and clearer instructions on how to activate and play their projects. This move—from having an "awareness of contributions"[55] to responding to the online community as an authentic audience and tool for learning—involves what education researcher Alicia Magnifico notes is critical thinking about communicating ideas to a group of people.[56]

Broadening Communities

Computational thinking and participation can be fostered and initiated in youth DIY online communities. Many programming and design tools (such as Alice, Gamestar Mechanic, and Kodu) include these types of communities[57] and create open-source sites (in the style of communities like Linux) for youth to share, comment on, and contribute to their coded creations. Others (such as the nonprofit education initiative Globaloria) have created hybrids that connect game design activities in schools to large national networks that provide community and support for student participants, teachers, and administrators.[58] The new version of Scratch 2.0[59] continues this trend by including features that allow users to share data at multiple levels. Through a virtual backpack, users can copy others' projects and store them for later use, and a Notes and Credits section helps fellow creators receive due credit when their work is repurposed. The 2.0 user profile pages are more customizable, and projects created through Scratch can be exported to social media sites.

Although affinity communities are not new (the pre-Internet Logo community is testament to this), even novice programmers now have an audience that values their artifacts and provides a potential community or affinity group. Tools that facilitate particular mechanics of programming are not enough. A social context is needed where these programming tools can be used and where programming artifacts are shared. In a 2005 investigation of Seymour Papert's samba schools, computer scientists José Zagal and Amy Bruckman analyze the characteristics of samba schools and highlight their flexibility to outsiders, the existence of a public event, and a plurality of members. The important message is that the success of the samba school relies not on the dance itself but on the social context in which the dance exists.

The Scratch website contains these three social elements. The site has a wide range of members and is open to new users. But as was learned from the Collab Challenge and Collab Camps within the Scratch site itself, there is a need for more explicit spaces or "public events" designated for sharing work constructively and collaboratively. The schools might be a viable potential partner for using online spaces for meaningful collaborations. Schools are ultimately social spaces, and the communal rules of classrooms offer children a viable model for learning how to share and cooperate online—particularly if teachers apply classroom rules to youth-based online environments like Scratch. When educators utilize Scratch and its online environment to support subject-matter learning, they bring their students online for a particular purpose, which itself can act as an event for grounding students' learning experiences.

Youth-based cooperation is never a guarantee, but it is more likely to develop in the presence of openness, diversity, and a unifying event. And such cooperation matters because learning how to program collaboratively results in more authentic and peer-based learning. Grasping the key elements of computational thinking—including decomposing a complex task into a series of interrelated modules and coordinating control flow between different project components—develops better work habits and facilitates a better baseline understanding of the nature systems. Computational thinking offers participants a model by which to parse the networked commons itself. Many data-mining tools rely on algorithms to search for and extract patterns from interactions and behaviors in massive communities. Likewise, tools like crowd-sourcing can leverage feedback from others, can be used to assess wider opinion, and can promote efficiency and reliability in applied programming activities.

5 From Scratch to Remix

Two paddles and a single multipixeled ball: these three modest objects have been hailed as the triumvirate that launched the entire video game industry. Although Pong *represents a rudimentary video game, its easy gameplay and competitive nature sparked a genuine fervor in dueling contestants throughout the 1970s and 1980s, and many played the interminable game for hours on end.[1]* Pong *has a revered and illustrious history in the gaming industry and has a minor history in Scratch. As one of the sample games that are highlighted in Scratch,* Pong's *familiarity makes it one of the first video games that Scratchers start playing and making using the Scratch software. Although* Pong *is simple to play (it has two paddles to move and a bouncing ball), designing your own DIY* Pong *is a more complex task that requires breaking down game play to its various "compartments" and making them work with one another. First, the programmer needs to program the ball movement (moving back and forth between the walls) and direction (going right or left) in addition to two paddles that can be controlled via the cursor or any other keys. In addition, sensory provisions need to be made if the ball hits the "edge" of a wall or a paddle as a condition for bouncing back. The seemingly simple task of moving a ball back and forth on a screen with two paddles provides a rich context for learning about looped behavior, conditional statements, and interface design.*

And just as the original video game launched hundreds of imitators, so has the remixable Scratch version birthed hundreds of Pong *variations. "3D Pong," "Beach Pong," and "World Cup Pong" all spin alternative and enhanced graphics on the original while also adding counters to keep track of score. "Pumpkin Pong" and "Santa Pong" celebrate the holidays. "Music Pong" creates a series of sound tones with each bounce of the ball that crescendo into minisongs. And "Pong ... Return of the Padell" adds an interactive storyline that, according to its Project Notes, narrates "An epic love story about a padell and a ball." Technical, playful, collegial, and even occasionally adversarial: this is the world of remix.*

Remix, the process of creating something new from something old,[2] follows the same pathway from the individual to the community that the previous chapter introduced. In the past, most programs had to be individually created "from scratch" to illustrate programming competencies, and code was understood to be a proprietary commodity that was built, refined, but certainly not shared. This approach set the tone for early computing coursework as children were introduced to the potential of programming in terms of input rather than output. Coursework focused on what children wrote as code rather than on what children actually produced with such code. The ability to build something "from scratch" or "from the ground up" under the "Language First" approach was the marker of a qualified programmer.[3] Yet this focus on individual input also had its pedagogical limitations. Akin to learning about writing fiction in a creative arts course by being taught the meaning of nouns, verbs, and modifiers, such computing pedagogy stressed text-based functionality over wider considerations, such as what the assembled text offered in terms of a discernible product.

In today's DIY culture, the term *scratch* takes on an altogether different meaning. Scratch software epitomizes this shift in meaning: the name derives from the "scratching" technique that was developed by hip-hop disc jockeys in the 1970s and 1980s.[4] Spinning and scratching vinyl records beside each other, these DJs juxtaposed and blended melodies and rhythms to create new harmonies. Their music was developed from snippets of wholly formed songs rather than from individual musical notes, and audiences responded enthusiastically, elevating remix from a little-known practice among likeminded DJs to an international phenomenon that today represents its own musical genre.

Remix has extended beyond music. In the field of computer programming, remix has a rich, if less widely known precedent. Within the technology industry, supervisors often develop the skills of novice programmers by having them tinker and build on existent pieces of code, which acquaints them with the language and gives them the opportunity to generate designs more complex than what they could accomplish solely on their own. Today repurposing code—or any digital media, for that matter—has taken on new meaning through the Internet. The emergence of Web 2.0 has allowed for unprecedented levels of making and sharing online to the extent that remix now represents a key practice in today's networked culture. "Creating" online today often means recreating and remixing by using Web-based venues to both download and upload digital content. In the vast online "middle ground," downloads are returned online as altered and often wholly new uploads. Although some view this middle ground with trepidation and see remix entirely in terms of intellectual property infringement, others herald remix as the essential lens by which individuals participate socially and economically[5] within an increasingly global society.

Given remix's meteoric ascent from a relatively obscure technical application to a process that is emblematic of what it means to create in the twenty-first century, where and how does remix start? Where do children learn to remix, and why is it appealing to them? What distinguishes remix from simply copying, and are there rules, both spoken and unspoken, that accompany the practice itself? Unfortunately (but perhaps unsurprisingly), these questions are not being addressed in most schools although children are having experiences with them "in the wild" at various content-sharing websites. Over the first half of this chapter, we examine how children are learning the practice of remix at the Scratch website, which currently represents the largest online collection of youth-oriented programmable remixes. What does remix look like in Scratch, and why do children choose to partake in the process? The other half of the chapter examines whether this increasingly popular practice can be integrated into schools and what kind of learning remix allows for in the classroom. What are the specific barriers for integration, and does the presence of these barriers outweigh the potential to make the learning of programming more authentic and collaborative? After all, computational participation is as much about learning the production of code as it is about the social practices and cultural norms in which it is embedded.

Why Remix? Exploring Motivations at the Scratch Website

Remixing has a significant presence on Scratch. According to a recent analysis of the projects uploaded to the site, over a quarter (27.64 percent or 670,932) of all projects at the website are remixes of previous projects.[6] Similar percentages of remixes have been reported on other youth-oriented programming sites, such as Kodu Game Lab and Studio Sketchpad.[7] To remix at Scratch is a simple process. When Scratchers open a project at the website and "look inside" at the underlying code, they are immediately presented with the option to remix via a button in the upper right-hand corner. When they click on the button, the project is reposted at the site as a remix. Thus, technically speaking, remixing at the Scratch site is easy.

Despite such technical ease, remix is taken seriously as a form of communal production online. Whenever an individual creates an account with Scratch, a crucial element of membership is agreeing to the open-source nature of the software, which is detailed in the Creative Commons Share-Alike license.[8] In addition to being constructive and respectful online, users are reminded by the Scratch management team that they also must be open to sharing online. They are free to remix any other project that they find at the Scratch website just as they can develop their own projects based on ideas and images that they find at the website. Users also must also be amenable to letting whatever they post online be downloaded by others. This includes the project itself and the underlying code that makes it operate.

The community guidelines also encourage members to give credit in their project notes section whenever a project is remixed.[9] This does not always happen, though. Whether by deliberate omission or a lack of understanding of remix protocol, Scratch members often repurpose and reupload projects that they find online without giving credit to the original creators. To address this lack of formal recognition, the Scratch team considered ways that attribution could be built into the site. Scratch researcher Andrés Monroy-Hernández added an automated attribution feature to the site that produced remix visualizations. This automated attribution allows users to track the development and repurposing of projects, which are now commonly referred to as "Scratch remix trees." Branching out on the screen like a family tree, these automated visualizations can be accessed with the click of a button, displaying all of the remixes of any single project (and whether the project itself is a remix) (figure 5.1).

By directly linking remixes to their antecedents based on the source code, these visualizations ensure that credit is given where credit is due.[10] Whether or not an individual user gives attribution to a fellow user in the project notes section, the remix tree is automatically generated, linking a project to the source metadata. This automatic attribution fosters a sense of fair play online, and the remix trees help facilitate the overall communal feel of the website. Although Scratch users appreciate and add to the community by friending each other, connecting on the Forums section, and adding "Love Its" to the projects that they most appreciate, remix trees highlight the communal nature of the website regardless of whether

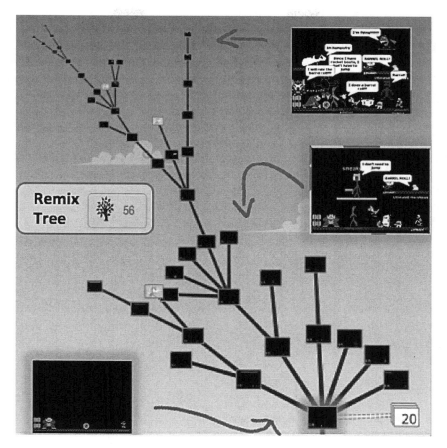

Figure 5.1
A remix tree for vortex19's project "Add Your Character Jumping While Somewhat Fitting Music Plays." The source project is highlighted at the bottom center of the remix tree as are two other projects along the remix chain. Clicking on any one of the fifty-six screens links to the individual remix.

individual users formally recognize such sociability. Common interests in terms of project content and coding scripts become more discernible with remix trees. The way that one attains a "high status" at the website also becomes more discernible because the projects that are at the "root" of remix tree "branches" (those that are most frequently remixed) are selected to appear on Scratch's highly coveted "front page" display, which has a "What the community is remixing" section among other categories.

Thus, individual status, communal goodwill, and overall productivity all play key roles in understanding why youth choose to remix each other's work at the Scratch website. But what do these remixes actually look like, and what coding schemes do they use? Do the look and feel of a remix vary based on the user's reasons for remixing? To answer these questions, it is helpful to return to media researcher Mizuko Ito and colleagues' categories of "hanging out," "messing around," and "geeking out" to explore why youth opt to use digital technologies.

Hanging Out: Remix as Socialization

As with Scratch collaborations that have been designed to involve as many participants as possible, one of the most basic forms of remix entails projects that were created to invite others to reuse and modify their code and images. The primary goal of these "hanging out" remixes is to invite others to join the project as a way to facilitate a joint social experience. What distinguishes "hanging out" in Scratch is that these "add on" projects often connect users who have never had any offline relationship. As is evident in the three examples in figure 5.2, the project titles tend to double as invitations and act as a basic, but fundamental, way to connect with others at the site. Although the code is altered in the process of adding another character, sound, or scene, such alteration usually entails accumulation and not revision. This type of remix tends not to change the existent code but builds on it with additional lines. Given that the goal is to generate connections through such remixes, it is important to be inclusive of what already has been added and what can be added. Altering another's code to change

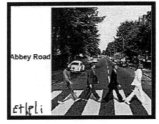

Figure 5.2
Three "hanging out" remixes: "Add Yourself as an Egg," "Add Yourself Jumping on a Trampoline," and "Add Yourself to Abbey Road."

an existing appearance or modify behavior may make ultimately for a more efficient project, but it also can be perceived as a direct challenge by other users, jeopardizing online relationships that are typically already tenuous based on minimal collaboration.

These forms of remixes can be considered wide in the sense that they reach a large number of contributors. In their extended reach, however, they are also far less deep in producing wholly coherent projects with clear storylines, consistent rules of play, and articulated end goals. Despite this lack of depth in terms of content and coding complexity, the project-based socializations that are seen with these remixes are inherently productive. Connecting through a remixable Scratch project involves more personal commitment and creativity than simply connecting via Facebook or Pinterest because sharing on Scratch—unlike these other two sites—relies on exchanging self-generated content.

Messing Around: Remix as a Pathway

These social remixes represent a crucial first step in introducing new users to the possibility of leveraging others' contributions to create something bigger and better. Although the Scratch website hosts projects that tap into television shows, movies, games, and books that are popular within youth culture, it can be daunting for young users to start using the software—particularly when they would like to generate their own interactive digital story or multilevel video game as their first foray into the Scratch community. Starting from the ground up is appealing to some new users but leaves other users unsure about where to start. These users are more interested in immersing themselves in already functional games, art, and stories than they are in working solely with the Scratch cat and a blank stage. By tinkering with existing Scratch content, new users have the satisfaction of maneuvering code that already has the semblance of a completed project while also putting their own unique spin on the project. Such tinkering also serves as an informal learning experience as new users frequently encounter Scratch blocks and scripts that allow for more complex project features (figure 5.3).

"I have to say if it weren't for remixing, I would have never understood velocity or scrolling," remarks fourteen-year-old Scratch member Chuck. But he also cautions that remix "should be used for things other than 'add

Figure 5.3
Three "messing around" remixes: "How to Scroll," "How to Use Variables (without Variables)," and "How to Make a Platform Game."

yourself' and coloring contests—not that I'm against those in any way. It's a tool that makes the Scratch community stand out as a friendlier and more learning-centered environment."[11] Chuck's point is insightful. Within Scratch, remixing has multiple purposes, but perhaps its greatest affordance is giving new users a foothold into learning to program as a means of exchange.

Documenting the various ways that Scratch users utilize remix as a pathway, educational researcher Karen Brennan notes that users often stumble onto remix as a way to learn.[12] She illustrates her point with the case of Nadia and Katie, two teenage users who ended up collaborating on an animated comics series that was based on remixing their own work. After she found a cache of static images at Katie's Scratch profile page, Nadia proposed animating these images into a series of digital shorts. Katie—who had no experience developing scripts and had never met Nadia before—agreed, and for a year and half the two girls from different countries exchanged images and scripts to produce ten episodes of a series entitled "Jodie the Superheroine." Through this series of remixes, Katie learned how to program in Scratch, and Nadia gained a better grasp of aesthetic expression and ways to thread together images to form a wholly cohesive animation. This series of remixing activities illustrates how social interaction can become the driving force for computational participation.

As is evident with Katie and Nadia's case, remix serves as the key practice for facilitating successful collaboration at Scratch and underpins the wider "community of practice"[13] in which all members agree to make their own work downloadable for the sake of increased productivity across the site. Perhaps nowhere is Scratch members' commitment to the wider community more evident than in a series of "how-to" projects that are posted for remix by the community. Created by individual users either alone or in collaboration with each other, these how-to projects (also referred to *tutorials* or *demos*) cover a range of project features, such as how to add a timer to a game and how to add velocity to a moving object. Although some how-to projects explain how to construct the relevant coding scripts step-by-step, other projects simply offer the script to remixers. The best how-to videos explain how to generate the script in the process of demonstrating it.

The project "How to Scroll," which was posted by Scratch user "cougers," is a good example of a project that exemplifies as it also explains. Scrolling is an essential element of console video games such as Super Mario Brothers and Pitfall. A moving background "scrolls" forward with the movement of the characters. Because scrolling is one of the most sought-after skills for Scratchers who are interested in making games, it leads the list of tutorials posted at the site. The "How to Scroll" project is popular (remixed ninety-four times) and has the player scroll forward along a shifting landscape in which the step-by-step instructions for generating the script appear along the horizon as one moves along. "It would be cool," posts its creator "cougers" in the Projects Notes section, "if this was turned into a game."

Through these various how-to tutorials, Scratch novices have the ability to create complex games, stories, and art projects in a relatively short amount of time—certainly far shorter than developing the project entirely from the ground up. The key factor is that these forms of remix do not just repurpose the individual coding bricks but take projects wholesale and combine them with each other to create entirely new projects. Within these "mega remixes," users are faced with the challenge of ensuring that the code from one project is compatible with the code from another project, and this can take considerable massaging on the part of the remixer. But after this is accomplished, the creator has built a project that functions on a series of complimentary "compartments" that exist in conjunction with each other and also function independently of the other, epitomizing what computer scientist David Parnas identifies as the crucial element of "information hiding" in his seminal paper on modular design in programming.[14] In remixing projects together as various modules, we see a potential for thinking and participating computationally—for creating more complex projects in shorter amounts of time based on a community of practice that is founded on a mutual agreement to remix respectfully.

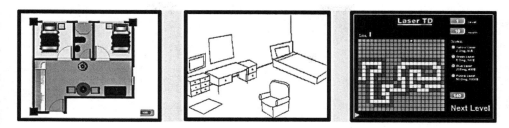

Figure 5.4
Three "geeking out" remixes: "The Roomba Remix Challenge," "Bedroom Maker," and "Laser Tower Defense."

The vacuum moves around the room at random while a timer (designating battery life) clicks at the bottom right. As the Roomba moves across the floor, it leaves a white pathway designating what has been cleaned. There are no controls for the user. In the Project Notes section, the project's creator explains the purpose of the project. "So what's the point, I hear you ask?" reads the Notes. "The point is to modify the programming logic in the Roomba to clean the floor more efficiently than the really dumb code that I supply is doing, before your battery runs flat." The author makes suggestions (such as ensure for better collision detection and even add logic to the machine) and explains that the project is "a game where you have to think about the programming, because a change to the program can take a few seconds but you have to wait several minutes as the vacuum does its job before you know how well you've done!"

Geared toward experienced Scratch programmers, the Roomba Remix Challenge is at the other end of the spectrum from the coloring contests. It requires tinkering, innovative thinking, and patience. The remixer has to conduct extended test runs of the vacuum each time to see if the revised code is making the device a more efficient cleaning agent. In their analysis of the social structures underpinning remix cultures, media scholars Giorgos Cheliotis and Jude Yew point to the significant role that is played by competitions in drawing new users to websites and in retaining interest and spurring motivation (and productivity) among experienced members.[18] This was our experience with the series of Scratch-based collaborative challenges sponsored at the website that are discussed in chapter 4.[19] Now entering into their fourth year, these collaborative initiatives start with a "seed project," which is a skeleton of a project and offers a basic framework (like a digital story or interactive art project) that entrants can use to remix in their respective teams. Remix sparks the collaborative activity and sustains this collaboration as the means to exchange projects through various states of revision.

Remix as Pedagogy: The Challenge and Possibility of Schools

A Cultural Challenge

Of all the characteristics of the aforementioned online Scratch remix challenges, three stand out as particularly effective in facilitating beginning programmers' learning. First, competing participants created with and for each other to produce games and stories that are personally meaningful to them. Second, these youth collaborated with their peers, acknowledging that what they did together could not be done as well alone. Third, they utilized remix as a means to revise and improve on their own work and the work of others. These three elements are aspects of learning that are rarely found in K–12 schools (and even in postsecondary education).[20]

First, in schools students typically do not produce their own content but summarize what others give them. Even when they produce their own work, they do so for their teacher and rarely for their peers. Second, even when classes entail collaboration, research has shown that group work is ineffective when a small minority of the group consistently takes on the majority of the responsibility while others do very little.[21] Accordingly, many students are disdainful of collaboration while others are too eager for it. Third, in schools, remix is not remix but more often considered outright plagiarism and is largely discouraged if not banned during the school day.

This third and final point makes clear the distinction between learning in the classroom and in DIY youth cultures such as Scratch online. Some may argue that the DIY culture of remix is antithetical to the institutional nature of K–12 schooling, where order and hierarchy tend to trump spontaneity as two of the core elements underpinning the overall educational system. Schools resist remix as a viable form of classroom-based production despite the growing number of media theorists and educators who posit remix as a new literacy[22] and the considerable research over the past decade on digital literacies.[23]

Such resistance comes from teachers, administrators, and students, who are sensitive about having their work appropriated by others—particularly without their explicit permission. In a 2010 study of how users react to having their projects remixed at the Scratch site, roughly a fifth left positive comments on their remixer's profile page, and a fifth accused the remixer of plagiarism. Participants reported that although the Remix Tree visualization helped demonstrate attribution, this alone did not curb such feelings of resentment because it was the computer rather than the actual individual giving attribution.[24] Sometimes the chance that work can be remixed at the Scratch site can be a hindrance rather than a help in encouraging youth to upload their work. For the first few weeks at an after-school club of middle-school students, nearly all members hesitated to post their projects online for fear that their work could be "high-jacked" by others.[25] Yet when the instructors explained that remix is a compliment, students changed their initial stance, on the whole, and understood and appreciated remix as a positive social gesture.

But even explaining remix as a compliment does not always assuage children's resistance. In "'No, I Don't Feel Complimented': A Young Artist's Take on Copyright," digital media researcher Dan Perkel describes his encounter with Sharon, a fifteen-year-old aspiring photographer who placed photographs online and discovered that they were copied onto several other websites. When asked if she considered such copy-and-paste appropriation to be a compliment, Sharon replied that she saw it as an intrusion upon her own work: "No, I don't feel complimented." Sharon removed the remainder of her pictures from online because she was unwilling to allow them to become available for remixing. "This kind of activity," writes Perkel, "deeply upset Sharon's sense of right and wrong." The ease with which her pictures could be accessed and appropriated led her to consider wider ethical considerations of remixing.

Embracing the Possibilities

Most K–12 schools promote a conception of copying that is at odds with the wider culture of remix, which results in a tension between the two groups. Yet this tension should lead schools to explore the benefits and dangers associated with remix. Although remixing on a basic level requires just a few mouse clicks to copy programs (and thus contributes little to computational thinking), selective remixing can require a high degree of sophistication and engage beginning designers in computational participation. Some remixing activities (such as considering what to modify in selected code segments, what to keep, and where to add or delete procedures or variables within a program) require a deep, functional understanding of the code, and in some instances, this type of remixing may be more complex than starting with a blank slate. Schools need to undertake and embrace the role of mediator. This can happen in two ways.

First and most immediately, schools need to address the nature of collaboration and the role of copyright since Web 2.0. On a political level, copyright in the digital domain (in code and interfaces) presents complicated issues that are being defined in light of new cultural practices.[26] For many youth, copyright is a complex issue to understand. The remixing dilemma[27]—the difficulty of promoting both originality and generativity in projects—suggests that remixing can deviate into being used as a crutch rather than as a spur for imaginative productivity. Yet addressing this question of remix as crutch or spur is a crucial question for twenty-first-century classrooms and can serve as an opportunity for examining copyright issues and addressing the social implications of computational participation, which often are neglected in the overt focus on technical prowess. Schools, researchers, and policy makers have made headway in this area, perhaps most notably with Harvard's GoodPlay project, which charts the ways that youth engage in ethical and moral issues as they engage with new media.[28]

With the increasing migration of reading, writing, and making of all kinds to online platforms, schools have to recognize the need for comprehensive reform. To this end, legal scholar Eric Perrott recommends implementing copyright education in all U.S. schools through the National Governors Association, and the Center for Social Media has posted online a series of best practices for teaching fair use in K–12 classes. These are admirable steps that focus on policies that inform K–12 curricula, but they avoid the question of pedagogy. Although there is interest in teaching children about the changing nature of what it means to create and re-create in the twenty-first century, schools lack meaningful practices for such lessons. Lecturing beside a white board is unlikely to help students understand what qualifies as fair use and copyright infringement—especially at the elementary and middle-school levels, where addressing issues of fairness is important developmentally. To do this effectively, educators need to create lessons that allow students to create remixable media, root those lessons in popular culture, and not simply talk about it.

Second, schools need to examine their own tendencies to operate in a top-down manner and give more credence to bottom-up approaches to learning. Educational theorists such as John Dewey and Ivan Illich have advanced theories about how national learning initiatives should best restructure themselves. In terms of addressing what it means to create within digital media, however, finding a place for a remix culture within the classroom represents a modest but crucial step toward making K–12 classrooms more collaborative spaces.

This does not require reinventing the wheel. Dewey's experiential education and Illich's notion of "learning webs" offer rich theoretical backdrops for remix as a pedagogical practice. There also exists pedagogical precedence (as discussed in chapter 2) in Sherry Turkle and Seymour Papert's notion of "bricolage," in which learners construct their own learning by "arranging and rearranging … a set of well-known materials" rather than simply receiving and reciting content that is given to them by the instructor.[29] Whereas traditional planning styles are inclined to view the process of problem solving as a matter of breaking down challenges from the top down into more digestible components, bricolage "describes problem solving as a conversation with the situation, in which the final solution emerges in the end."[30]

In terms of learning programming through remix, a number of initiatives utilize bricolage—most notably computer science education researcher Betsy DiSalvo and colleagues' Glitch Game Testers initiative through the Georgia Institute of Technology and Morehouse College.[31] Started in 2009, Glitch Game Testers introduces African American high school boys to computation and interface design by having them test prerelease video games from EA Games and other popular gaming companies. Searching out "bugs" in gameplay, students identify problems in game design and play and make notes for remixed revisions for the participating company.

This element of bricolage via remix is also evident with the development and use of a series of Scratch-based puzzles entitled "Debug'ems" that are posted at the Scratch site.[32] These projects are designed to include an error and require the user to find a solution. Whether it is repairing a clock counter in a game or finetuning a sprite's sensory capacity, these projects utilize sampling and remix to reverse-engineer the construction process, much like the Roomba Remix Challenge.

Developing a Culture of "Deep Shareability"

Youth are constantly looking at one another's projects, trading ideas, sharing techniques. To fit into this context, the object architecture of Scratch supports what we call "deep shareability."
—John Maloney et al., "Scratch: A Sneak Preview"[33]

The term *shareability* represents what it means for children to operate socially in the time of Web 2.0. Young people socialize by sharing content on Facebook, Twitter, Instagram, Pinterest, and other social media. But this notion of "deep shareability" that Scratch's lead designer John Maloney and his colleagues refer to in the quote above goes beyond posting photos and "liking" other people's pictures on Facebook. When young people collaborate on a programmed project, solicit feedback online, and welcome others to remix their work, sharing entails real communication, cooperation, and production—all three of which come together in the practice of remix.

According to legal scholar Yochai Benkler, we live in a world that increasingly relies on "commons-based peer production" in which altruism is not simply a moral imperative but an economic one. New media theorist Vito Campanelli states that remix is a process that is deeply ingrained in people and that it is "an evolutionary duty, arising from every human's innate need to personally transform the materials available to them."[34] Within the psychology of creativity, conceptual combinations, especially combinations in new and unexpected ways, drive new ideas.[35]

It is difficult to predict how much schools, as institutions that can drive new ideas, will embrace remix as a practice and pedagogy because schools are following wider industry standards, which wield copyright law to stifle remix rather than encourage it. Another model for remix is the growing open-source movement, which encourages a conception of software not as property but as information.[36] Yet for this open-source movement to gain traction and for schools to deliver on their promise as places of new ideas, remix must be taught and practiced in classrooms.

6   From Screens to Tangibles

In spring 2012, the grassroots crowd-funding website Kickstarter listed a new request for funding. Two MIT students, Jay Silver and Eric Rosenbaum, were looking for funding for a computational construction kit called MaKey MaKey. The opening text teased potential backers by asking "Ever played Mario on Play-Doh or piano on bananas? Alligator clip the Internet to your world and start inventing the future." By clipping one alligator clip to the MaKey MaKey board and another one to a conductive object (such as an apple, a banana, or aluminum foil), the user closes a circuit. When users touch the selected object, they manipulate programmed behavior on the Scratch screen. As the "invention kit for the 21st century," MaKey MaKey invites users to rediscover the computational potential of ordinary objects in everyday life by transforming them into touchpads and combining them with the Internet. As an invention kit, MaKey MaKey is simple enough for beginners and yet complex enough for professional artists and engineers to use in their own respective trades. Jay and Eric's request for startup funding was accompanied by a video clip that illustrated various MaKey MaKey projects. Within a few days, the campaign reached its initial goal of the $25,000 that was required to kickstart the project, but the money and the feedback did not stop. Hundreds of questions and ideas of what MaKey MaKey could do and what one could make with it filled the comment pages long before anyone received a kit. People asked whether it allowed Bluetooth connectivity, whether one could connect two MaKey MaKeys to a keyboard, and whether applications could ease movement and open access for children with disabilities and senior citizens. By the end of the campaign, over eleven thousand backers had signed up for a package and provided $586,106 in startup funding. It was one of the most successful Kickstarter campaigns of the year and attracted nearly twenty-four times the amount of funding that its inventors initially requested.[1]

At one time, electronic construction kits were sold to a few dedicated hobby-ists who were interested in building their own airplanes and ham radios. But Kickstarter campaigns have raised startup money for several computational construction kits. Like Makey Makey, those campaigns were built around the open-source Arduino board and software and allowed customization for particular activities (such as designing a robot) or provided a Scratch-style interface for programming different open hardware platforms. But MaKey MaKey was unique because it was able to make tangible computation read-ily accessible. Most of the MaKey MaKey projects that were featured in the promotional video for Kickstarter could be designed by connecting the alli-gator clips to preset ports on the MaKey MaKey board, and none required previous programming experience. Like Scratch, MaKey MaKey provides low thresholds for beginners and high ceilings for advanced designers. Finally, MaKey Makey was affordable. The board cost less than $50, well under the price of the Lego Mindstorms kits, which can cost hundreds of dollars. This trend toward accessible, tangible, computational construction kits is continuing. Why simply program robots and racecars when you can take the pillows from your couch, the keys to your car, and the door to your room and make them programmable and playable? In 2012, the African Robotics Network launched a challenge to design a $10 robotics kit so that children all over the world could learn to make their own programmable robots and identified several winning designs.[2]

MaKey MaKey is not a stand-alone application. It taps into growing online communities that have formed around the open-source Arduino board.[3] Not unlike the Scratch community that is described in chapter 4, Arduino-based applications have spurred entire do-it-yourself communities whose members share their creations online, offer tutorials and technical support, and leverage the Web to create spaces for like-minded enthusiasts. At the online community Instructables, for example, hundreds of thou-sands of entries provide information and video documentation on how to build or fix nearly anything. The hobbyist culture is part of the larger DIY or maker movement that is bringing back manual crafts, promot-ing local manufacturing, and providing access to digital fabrication with three-dimensional printers and laser cutters in Fab Labs. The launch of *Make* magazine in 2005 and the annual Maker Faires across the country shortly thereafter has created a national forum and local meeting places to share and celebrate DIY designs.[4] The success of MaKey MaKey's Kickstarter campaign and others reveals that a broad audience is interested in making things that can be programmed and be played with in the physical world.

The maker movement is not limited to the informal spaces of clubs and homes but is expanding into educational spaces in museums, libraries, and schools. Science centers and museums across the country are setting up maker spaces in their halls. The New York Hall of Science, the Exploratorium, and the Lawrence Hall of Science were among the first to experiment with this new model of interactivity with their patrons. Now visitors come to see and interact with exhibits and also might make something linked to the exhibit theme. Public libraries in Chicago, Philadelphia, and elsewhere are expanding their focus from books to teen spaces where young users can access computers to search information, complete their homework, play games, and engage in digital production of animations, games, and electronic textiles.[5] The MakerEd initiative has developed and deployed a Maker Corps—young people who are interested in assisting other youth and communities with DIY projects. The Boy Scouts of America added a game design merit badge in 2013, a programming badge, and a computer-aided design badge in 2014. Will being able to design and program digital media soon be a fundamental scouting skill, like lighting a fire or charting a path in the woods? In the thicket of Web-based media, these may well be the new wilderness survival skills. Schools are recognizing the potential of programming in the design and construction of physical objects and are beginning to set up what computer science educators Ann and Mike Eisenberg envisioned to be a new and improved shop class that interweaves computation and material science in computer-enriched handicrafts.

This move of educational technology beyond the computer screen to meld the digital with the tangible is the focus of this chapter. Much of what is discussed in previous chapters—interactive digital stories, video games, animations, and massive online communities—is located on stationary computer screens. As sociologist Sherry Turkle once remarked, much of our digital life now seems to happen on the screen and not in the physical world. But mobile technologies with small and portable screens have brought this physical side of computing into our everyday lives. And they have made the design of tangible technologies accessible and affordable to all users. This interest in tangibles may be an early indication that the pendulum is swinging back: what started out as a migration from in-person to screen-to-screen interactions is shifting back to a hands-on-and-with-others mode.

In the remaining sections of this chapter, we review the success of robotic construction kits and competitions. Robotics successfully gained a foothold in the unoccupied school space of computing, but to cast a wider net in engaging children, educators and researchers have suggested opening up new clubhouses that engage in computational activities besides robots—such as designing electronic textiles and tangible interfaces. A common thread in these sections is how simple tweaks in technology designs can create new communities or clubhouses, an important finding for improving learning opportunities and generating more equitable access to computational participation.

Playing in the Clubhouse: Lego Mindstorms

Computational construction kits like MaKey MaKey always have had a special place in constructionism. In 1980, the cover of the first edition of Seymour Papert's book *Mindstorms: Children, Computers, and Powerful Ideas* featured a girl with a large robotic turtle on the floor.[6] The early Logo turtle was a physical object, not a screen object. It was programmed to move on the floor and, using a pen attached to its bottom, to draw designs and images on a piece of paper. Both the programmer and the onlooker could easily replicate the physical movement of the turtle with their own bodies. This might seem to be insignificant in terms of learning, but by being able to mimic the programmed movement of turtle, children could more easily comprehend the abstract input and execute commands. These tangible aspects of learning were ignored at the time, but today many educational researchers see cognition as embodied. For them, thinking and learning are embodied in objects, gestures, and interactions and not only in the mind. Papert's idea of body-syntonic learning was one of representation and pedagogy. Although many efforts focused on developing programming tools for beginning programmers (see chapter 4), a parallel strand of research was developing computational construction kits (such as Lego/Logo and Pico) that allowed people to build their own robotic turtles and many other creations. These efforts eventually grew into a commercial industry. The popular Lego Mindstorms kits, for example, can be purchased at most museum gift shops and toy stores.

In the early stages of designing Lego/Logo, computer scientist Mitchel Resnick and toy designer Steven Ocko described it as a tool for animating and controlling Lego objects with engines and sensors.[7] Designers wrote programs on the computer, and those programs were used to command the sensors and engines in Lego objects that were tethered to the computer via long cables. Lego objects could navigate mazes on their own and no longer needed to be moved by hand. Sensors that reacted to light, touch, and sound could be programmed to react to the environment, adjust behavior accordingly, and display alternative behavior. Later developments such as the programmable brick removed the cable tethers by downloading the programs into a small computer that could be combined with Lego bricks (figure 6.1).

As Mitchel Resnick, Fred Martin, Randy Sargent, and Brian Silverman proposed, Lego/Logo and the programmable brick could become toys-to-think-with in the design of interactive environments—such as alarm clocks that tilt beds to stir late morning sleepers, miniature Ferris wheels that spin in intervals, or dolls that periodically blink their eyelids. The programmable brick could turn it into a behavior construction kit. Young designers could design autonomous creatures that mimicked the actions of living animals by programming simple behaviors, such as retracting the head or moving backward when the turtle hit a wall. Finally, they could use the programmable bricks to construct scientific instruments, such as a miniature pedometer that records a pet hamster's nightly running patterns in its cage. In each of these cases, young designers engineered Lego structures that could be animated with machines and controlled with sensors and also wrote program commands defining the conditions under which particular actions would be executed. This is no small feat. Coordinating these imagined designs and built systems is challenging even for undergraduate engineering students. This was documented by computer science educator Fred Martin when he examined undergraduates' design approaches, technical solutions, and learning of engineering and programming in designing robots for competitions.

The change from the name Lego/Logo[8] to Lego Mindstorms intentionally referenced Papert's book title *Mindstorms* (figure 6.2). It left the MIT Media Lab, where many early prototypes were developed, and became commercially available. The boxes provide sensors, engines, and the familiar Lego bricks, which could be used to build robots and interactive houses and

Figure 6.1
Lego TC Logo (top) and Lego Mindstorms box (bottom). Photos courtesy of The Lego Group.

rebuild and animate robots from the popular Star Wars movie franchise. Robotic technologies and materials that previously were available only to students in college classes and university labs were now accessible and relatively affordable for schools and families. Programming instruction in terms of Basic, Logo, and Pascal had long been abandoned by school computer labs, so learning programming and engineering via robotics entered through the backdoor of afterschool clubs. Over the years, afterschool robotics clubs became one of the few places in many K–12 schools where programming and engineering found a home, but this home was consistently outside the standard curriculum.

Robotics in K–12 also brought with it a new model for displaying and sharing designs—competitions. These competitions grew out of January robotics classes at MIT that gave engineering students hands-on experience in actual soldering and building physical things during the intersession period.[9] Each robotics class culminated in a public competition in a large auditorium filled with cheering students. Challenges were often mundane tasks, such as gathering scattered ping-pong balls and moving them to the other side of a table. But given that the robot was the sole actor on the stage, these everyday tasks took considerable forethought and revision on the part of the engineering teams.

Robotics competitions have become science fairs with a new edge, providing public exposure and authentic audiences for typical robot design challenges (such as building a tower, running through a maze, or collecting ping-pong balls and moving them to the other side of a table). The FIRST (For Inspiration and Recognition of Science and Technology) Lego League meetings started in 1992, and now high schools from all over the country and across the world participate at local, regional, and national levels.[10] A recent study conducted by Brandeis University and commissioned by the FIRST Lego League reported positive influences on participants' attitudes, skills, knowledge of science and technology, and sense of self-confidence.[11] Furthermore, participation in these activities, often motivated by teachers' or parents' encouragement, was highly correlated with later career choices in science, technology, engineering and mathematics (STEM) majors.

Although the robotics competitions are now considered an established and in many places the only part of creative computing and engineering cultures in K–12 schools, they have not reached everyone. They have been only marginally successful in increasing the participation of girls and

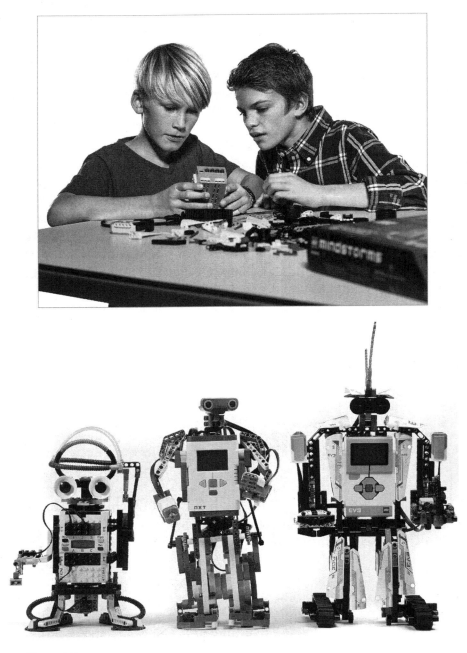

Figure 6.2
Boys playing with Lego Mindstorms (top) and examples of robots (bottom). Photos
courtesy of The Lego Group.

minorities. In academic year 2008–2009, 7,800 teams participated in the FIRST Lego League robotics competition, and 70 percent of youth participants were boys and white. This finding seems to reflect the equally marginal participation of girls and underrepresented groups in science fairs, especially in physical, earth, and math or computer science projects.[12] In addition, robotics teams are limited to how many students can participate, so the activities do not easily scale up. Paying for materials and for travel to robotics competitions is expensive, often requiring schools to conduct extensive fundraising events to finance afterschool robotics programs and participation in out-of-state competitions.

Finally, the competitions are an audience for the learning project. Although building robots in response to specific design challenges is a rich learning and collaboration experience,[13] the winner-takes-it-all approach that is promoted in competitions might not appeal to some people. Competitions provide an authentic and rewarding audience, but judging by the growing number of online competitions, they seem to have become the default audience for all digital media designs judging. The STEM National Video Game Design Challenge and dozens of others have become the central outlet for game designs in schools.[14] Although competitions provide a valuable audience, they cannot and should not be the only outlet that can engage youth in computational participation, especially if we know about their rather limited track record in reaching out and broadening participation.

Many afterschool programs and community technology centers and organizations have done the job that K–12 schools have failed to do in terms of introducing the creative power of computing. But too many of these clubhouses fail to broaden participation in the discipline and instead mirror the geek clubs that many see as the face of computing. What if organizations created new clubhouses with different materials and activities rather than aim to bring everyone into the existing model? This is exactly the question that computer scientist Leah Buechley and others asked and answered when they set out to develop a new category of computational construction kits that involved textiles instead of bricks and crafting in addition to engineering.

Opening New Clubhouses: Electronic Textiles

Textile construction kits, also called electronic textiles (e-textiles), are a fairly recent development. E-textiles are programmable garments, accessories, and costumes that incorporate elements of embedded computing that allow the behavior of fabric artifacts to be controlled. Designing e-textiles can involve novel materials (such as conductive fibers or Velcro), sensors for light and sound, actuators (such as LEDs and speakers), and traditional aspects of textile crafts. One popular e-textile construction kit is LilyPad Arduino,[15] which enables novice engineers and designers to embed electronic hardware into textiles (figure 6.3).

To make an e-textile, designers sew LilyPad modules together with conductive thread and employ the popular Arduino or ModKit development environments to program the LilyPad microcontroller to manage sensor and output modules (like LEDs) in their designs. Since its commercial release in 2007, LilyPad Arduino has been widely adopted by designers and engineers of all ages from around the world and employed in a number of universities in computer science, engineering, fine arts, and design courses. E-textiles can be considered a part of a larger DIY movement to promote personalized fabrication outside of traditional manufacturing that can also extend into classrooms, as the following examples from an e-textile high school class illustrate (figure 6.4).

What do people learn when they craft e-textile designs? Students learn about sewing and other types of crafting that often is found in vocational education or leisure time but usually not in the context of traditional school topics such as science and mathematics. In addition, students learn about engineering when they design functional circuits by connecting alligator clips to batteries, switches, and LEDs; align polar ends of LEDs; knotting thread ends; and sewing these to fabric. Students also learn how to program and remix Arduino code, which controls and executes the desired behaviors of sensors and actuators, thus providing a context for engaging with computational concepts and practices.[16]

Leah Buechley, who invented the LilyPad Arduino, argues that such design learning makes transparent the different layers and connections of technology that are often hidden in the commercially available technologies that come in shiny cases and reveal little about their underlying

Figure 6.3
LilyPad Arduino and components: A turn signal jacket (top) and sewing with con- ▶
ductive thread (middle right) and LilyPad, sensors, and battery holder (middle left). A group of students at an e-textile workshop at the Franklin Institute (bottom). Photos by Eunkyoung Lee.

Figure 6.4
E-textile designs by high school students: A cupcake cushion that lights up when pressed (top left), a sunflower shirt in which LEDs sparkle when a button is pushed (top right), a music boom box that plays music when two patches are pressed (bottom left), and an octopus toy that lights up (bottom right). Below each photo is a diagram of the circuit design that connects the LilyPad Arduino with actuators such as LEDs, sound buzzers, and sensors made of conductive fabric. Photos by Eunkyoung Lee.

functionalities.[17] This call for transparency illustrates an important pedagogical dimension of tangible computing, one that Papert stressed with the
body syntonicity of the turtle. It was a matter of representation (being the
turtle on the floor or on the screen), touch (touching circuits), and pedagogy (understanding the functionality and building personal connections
to the objects). Working across different domains—crafting, engineering,
and computing—underscores the importance of seeing how concepts cross
a range of media and conditions.

But there is a second, equally important dimension of transparency that
relates to bringing together different cultures—crafting and sewing (which
historically are associated with women) and engineering and computing
(which historically are associated with men). We observed in numerous
workshops and classes how these references to the gendered nature of e-textile materials and activities slip into conversations. When middle-school
boys label their activities "doing circuits" rather than sewing or when
high school boys talk about "sewing being a girl's sport," they are claim-
ing that engineering is more valuable and more appropriate for males.[18]
On the other side, some argue that learning with e-textiles reinforces existing gender stereotypes and that women should participate in more male-
dominated activities, like robotics. Such tensions are productive because
they open up conversations and question fairly narrow perceptions about
computation.

The LilyPad Arduino e-textile construction kit harks back to longstanding historical connections between women, textiles, and computing. Ada
Lovelace's notes on the analytical engine resulted in the first "computer
program" in the nineteenth century, and the Jacquard loom, which used
punched cards to weave complex patterns in textiles, is considered by many
the first step in the history of computing hardware. Lovelace wrote perhaps
the most beautiful sentence ever to link fashion and computing: "We may
say most aptly that the Analytical Engine weaves algebraic patterns just
as the Jacquard loom weaves flowers and leaves."[19] Cultures of computing moved from textile weaving to code crunching during war and now
are returning to crafting, gaining new impetus from digital fabrication.
E-textile construction kits make visible the complex intersection of culture
and computing because they bring together domains that are seen as con-
tradictory. Their existence provides a visible counterargument by bringing
together the low- and high-tech forms of computing.

They also allow students to see that simple design modifications can connect the same technologies with very different communities. The Lily-Pad Arduino's sensors and actuators are modifications of the functionally equivalent Arduino board, sensors, and actuators. This means that the LilyPad Arduino can do anything that the Arduino board can do and vice versa. Yet we know from a recent study by Leah Buechley and Benjamin Mako Hill[20] that many more women participate in the LilyPad community than in the Arduino community: of projects posted on the Web, 80 percent of Arduino projects were completed by male designers, and 80 percent of LilyPad Arduino projects were completed by female designers. Although robotic kits like Lego Mindstorms invite a certain kind of computational production and producers, so do textile construction kits like the LilyPad Arduino. The design and framing of computational activities and materials affects who sees themselves as part of the community and then joins and participates in it.

Likewise, the communal sewing circles that are the design context for many e-textile activities are unlike the competition-driven workshops of the robotic activities. Competitions have an energizing function, providing purpose and audience in a shared event, but they should not be the only model for organizing, presenting, and celebrating computational participation. We need to create new communities that, unlike the robotics competition, provide a collaborative and supportive atmosphere. We are building such new communities and events around computational crafting activities. Called eCrafting Circles,[21] they intentionally refer to the quilting bees and sewing circles that used to bring together neighbors to produce quilts, clothes, and more (see figure 6.3 bottom). Rather than competitions, online crafting circles will be time-sensitive, locally relevant events that allow for sharing and displaying of computational crafts. These are intended to spark increased participation and collaboration in e-textiles, similar to the way FIRST Lego League competitions have increased participation in robotics, but without the emphasis on competition that deters significant groups of people from joining.[22] Scalable across regions while adaptable to local needs, eCrafting Circles are intended to provide a forum that allows like-minded and interested participants to share learned insights and provide much needed support for their designs. Much of computational participation has focused on the online world, but there is equal benefit to be found in physical construction and local participation. We might want to revisit what computer labs and classes could look like when crafting and computing provide new materials, activities, and audiences for learning.

Shop Classes for the Next Millennium: Animated Pop-Up Books, Game Arcades, and Public Displays

In new clubhouses, community centers, and afterschool programs, students will be able to interact with computers to communicate, receive, and organize information. But new clubhouses cannot bear the sole responsibility for teaching children to think systematically and creatively using computers. School classrooms need to embrace the hands-on, creative technical learning that has been fostered in peripheral clubs. In the vocational education and industrial arts courses of the 1950s, students used technology collaboratively and constructively in real-life applications. By the 1970s, however, some reformers were characterizing such classes as pointless or unchallenging, even though they made education more hands-on, practical, and project-driven and represented some of the most innovative thought in education, particularly the progressive ideas of John Dewey in *Experience and Education.*[23]

The promise of hands-on and creative learning through technology has not been forgotten. More than a decade ago, computer scientists and educators Mike and Ann Eisenberg envisioned a next generation of shop classes that would include computational media and crafts—what they called computer-enriched handicrafts.[24] Shop classes, which often are taken by students who are not going on to college, can engage all learners in designing and understanding technology by blending computation and material artifacts. This reevaluation of the concrete for learning has also been supported by education writer Mike Rose, who has analyzed the intellectual dimensions of trades, crafts, and arts. Most educational research has focused on understanding learning and teaching in academic disciplines such as science, mathematics, and language arts and has paid little attention to the intellectual demands and opportunities found in plumbing, carpentry, and waitressing. Yet building robots and crafting electronic textiles are compelling illustrations of how crafting, engineering, and computer science can generate rich and engaging learning contexts.

One unexpected direction for next-generation shop classes has been a return to paper and paint, enhanced with conductivity and computation.

Although digital learning has moved away from the printed text that has been the foundation of literacy for hundreds of years, computational design and paper crafts can be merged in innovative ways. For instance, Mike and Ann Eisenberg's HyperGami allows students to use origami paper folding crafts, computation, and geometry to design three-dimensional objects on the screen that can be printed out and folded into paper creatures and objects (figure 6.5). Pop-up books can embed circuitry with LEDs that light up when pages are opened or paper strips are pulled. Although these activities do not require coding, they are a first step into the world of making connections in circuits that can be enhanced with programming. The work on paper can be further expanded to include conductive paint that can animate information on the page or connect back to a computer screen. Many of these projects have tackled the conceptual and technical challenges of designing materials and tools, and they now become accessible for learning and teaching the next-generation shop class.

Computer scientist Amon Millner's pioneering work with Hook-Ups illustrates how youth can learn about electricity, design, and programming while crafting tangible interfaces with everyday and found materials. MaKey MaKey, discussed at the beginning of this chapter, is a low-cost computational construction kit that has lowered the barriers for setting up computational-style shop classes (figure 6.6). What if game design activities can be extended into the material world with the joystick interfaces that are found in popular gaming consoles and arcades? In the 1970s and 1980s, gaming arcades were lively and public spheres that provided many youths with their first access to video games. More recently, we worked with a class of middle-school students who set up an arcade with remixed Scratch games and touchpad designs. Although the banana piano keyboard was compelling in the video, it turned out to be less practical in classroom settings. Play-Doh—a malleable, reusable, and conductive mass—became the material of choice for students who were designing tangible game interfaces that incorporated both aesthetic and functional elements. Some students matched their controller components to the character sprites in their video games, and others used the Play-Doh to represent the directions in which the sprites in the games could move.

Everyone spent significant effort on redesigning Scratch games, drawing or downloading new sprites (characters), designing custom backgrounds, modifying existing sprites, and adding sound effects, all while attending

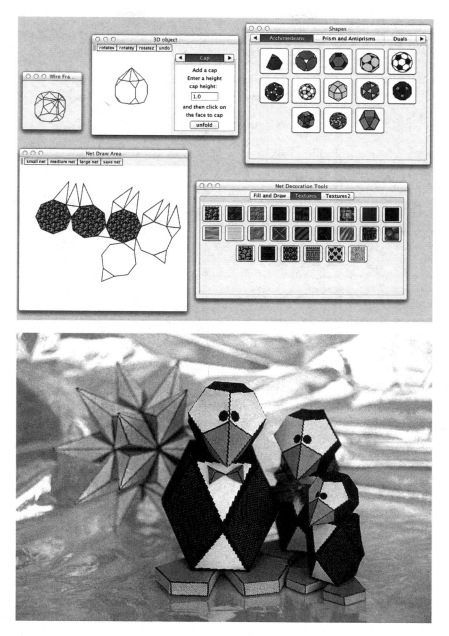

Figure 6.5
The HyperGami interface (top) and a family of penguin paper sculptures (bottom).
Photos by Ann and Mike Eisenberg.

Figure 6.6
MaKey MaKey designs of game interfaces (top) and musical instruments (bottom) on Scratch Day at Penn 2013. Photos courtesy of Darryl Morgan Photography.

to usability conventions such as adding scores, adding bad guys or distractors, and adding a way to win or end the game. Designing the touchpads also introduced material requirements that are absent from the world of computer screens. Some youths struggled to ensure that the alligator clips remained in their Play-Doh touch pads. For others, the Play-Doh controllers leaked moisture onto background paper, creating short circuits that required them to be maintained as separate pieces instead of one touch pad.

Situating the game designs in an arcade rather than in a competition provided an attentive audience for the game designs and a rich learning experience. The arcade experience became a lesson in debugging and rapid prototyping as an array of challenges came up: alligator clips fell out of controllers, controller pieces fell to the ground, and participants realized that they needed to adjust their game by adding scores so that more people could play. Several designers made numerous small fixes to ensure the integrity of their controllers and added conductive bracelets and touch pads to make more obvious that players needed to touch the earth clip for the interfaces to function properly. They also gained some valuable insights about design and usability from seeing others play their game and make real-time adjustments. Using Play-Doh as a conductive material to make tangible game interfaces turned out to be a rich learning experience, much like working with conductive thread to make e-textiles.

Creating audiences for displaying, testing, and enjoying the handmade and coded artifacts is an important dimension of constructionist learning and teaching. Computer scientists Mike Eisenberg and Sherry Hsi's latest project, Math on a Sphere, presents yet another twist on computational participation (figure 6.7). This project uses large spherical displays that were developed by the National Oceanic and Atmospheric Administration and are used in many science centers to show graphics and animations. In a Logo-like programming environment, children can create their own designs as they learn about non-Euclidian geometry and coding. The oversized dimensions of the Walk-Through Computer inspired visitors to think about the functionality of the machine, and in a similar manner, the gigantic displays of Math on a Sphere engage young designers to see themselves as programming for an audience, albeit distant. Although access to these displays is currently available only in the Lawrence Hall of Science and the Fiske Planetarium at the University of Colorado at Boulder, this idea could be expanded to more public centers. It provides another avenue

Figure 6.7
A three-dimensional display: Math on a Sphere. Photos by Antranig Basman (top) and Sherry Hsi (bottom).

for thinking about where the audience is and how it can be reached and for broadening our perceptions of what computational participation can mean. In designing artifacts for public display and performance, students find that objects-to-think-with become objects-to-share-with, demonstrating the communal relevance of what is learned, much as the carnival provides dancers with an audience and a purpose for learning and practicing dances all year round.

Making as Learning

Ann and Mike Eisenberg and many others envision a new set of shop classes that teach about game controller designs, paper crafts, electronic textiles and sensors, and interactive environment designs. FIRST Lego Mindstorms, LilyPad Arduino, and MaKey MaKey are part of a movement that is starting to make computational construction kits available to the larger public. These construction kits add dimensions to learning and understanding that have been overlooked in education, leaving students with few tangible artifacts of their academic work that can travel home and in time with them. Such physical connections between school and home are common in the elementary grades, but they seem largely forgotten after students move into the more abstract domains of science and mathematics at the high school level. The new maker spaces and fabrication laboratories (fablabs) have three-dimensional printers and laser cutters and blend together computing, crafting, and material science.

These new spaces and clubhouses are places where members can use embedded computation to create fashion and soft objects. The extension of computation into the tangible world allows students to engage with new materials and new activities that can help them broaden their computational participation. For marginalized young people who have been left out of the computing pipeline, such domain-crossing activities capitalize on and affirm their interests in low-tech materials while simultaneously introducing new content. The mind-and-hand merger of the digital and physical repositions youth as active creators rather than just consumers of knowledge. These new tangible forms of computing also provide a more nuanced understanding of how technology works with a broader range of materials that is crucial for today's DIY citizenship, as more aspects of life move into the digital domain.

Cultivating understanding of technology on both conceptual and material levels is important for several reasons. On a general level, it promotes understanding of the basic functionalities that underlie the designs of interfaces, systems, and materials. These understandings also empower learners on a political level by providing them with resources to question the decisions and designs that are made by others. Finally, on a personal level, using and making technologies for expressive purposes help students to communicate better and build relationships. Learning how to work with materials at the intersection of programming and engineering is no small feat. The robotics courses are time intensive, learning with e-textiles requires many different skills, and teacher and mentor support in and out of class is essential to help make these tangibles become real and alive, which is the focus of the next chapter.

7 Connected Teaching

Imagine a party of time travelers from an earlier century, among them one group of surgeons and another of schoolteachers, each group eager to see how much things have changed in their profession a hundred or more years into the future. Imagine the bewilderment of surgeons finding themselves in the operating room of a modern hospital. Although they would know that an operation of some sort was being performed, and might be guess at the target organ, they would in almost all cases be unable to figure out what the surgeon was trying to accomplish or what the purpose of the many strange devices he and the surgical staff were employing. The rituals of antisepsis and anesthesia, the beeping electronics, and even the bright lights, all so familiar to television audiences, would be utterly unfamiliar to them.

The time-traveling teachers would respond very differently to a modern elementary school classroom. They might be puzzled by a few strange objects. They might notice that some standard techniques had changed—and would likely disagree among themselves about whether the changes they saw were for the better or the worse—but they would fully see the point of most of what was being attempted and could quite easily take over the class.[1]

This tale from Seymour Papert's 1993 book, *The Children's Machine: Rethinking School in the Age of the Computer*, is an anecdote with many variations. Another version features Rip Van Winkle, who awakes from his twenty-year nap and finds the only semblance of modern life similar to that of his past to be the inside of classrooms; another version features a middle-school classroom serving as a time capsule for generations of students. And such tales are rooted in a certain truth: whether it is a blackboard, white board, or Smartboard on the wall, the rows of desks have been facing it since U.S. public school's inception. Of all the spaces in society, school classrooms have changed very little over the centuries. This was Papert's sentiment at the time *The Children's Machine* was published in 1993. Opening the book with a chapter entitled "Yearners and Schoolers," Papert distinguishes between reformists who are committed to revisioning schooling (the yearners) and those who generally accept the educational status quo (the schoolers). The book serves as the follow-up to Papert's 1980 *Mindstorms: Children,*

Computers, and Powerful Ideas, to the extent that it addresses Logo's rise and fall in schools, which Papert attributes to the schools' resistance to change.

"There are only two things wrong with schools," quips cognitive psychologist, Roger Schank: "What we teach and how we teach it,"[2] and it is easy to be cynical about education today, particularly with the increasing number of alternative educational opportunities available, offline and online. The role played by digital technologies in education may be the most polarizing issue facing teaching pedagogy these days, with some people denouncing Web-based media as the downfall of modern education and others heralding such media as the single-handed savior of it. This chapter aims to find a middle ground between these two views and between the yearners and schoolers by reconceptualizing what it means to learn and teach technological fluency in the twenty-first century but also by appreciating the importance of working within the strictures and dynamics characteristic of K–12 classrooms. This is not an easy middle ground to find. A common theme across the previous six chapters has been the challenge of bringing the scrappy, do-it-yourself culture that is characteristic of coding circles like Scratch, among others, into the realm of schooling. Institutional schooling and these much looser, informal learning networks appear to be at odds with each other, and as chapter 5 points out, this tension comes to a head with certain digital media practices such as remix, which one community largely embraces as a creative impulse and the other frequently dismisses as cheating.

Yet for computing and technology education[3] overall, finding a middle ground between yearners and schoolers is important because both groups have much to gain by compromise. Schoolers gain by creating classrooms that are more open and dynamic spaces that allow for greater student creativity and collaboration using technology. Yearners gain by achieving legitimacy—by moving from the relatively confined spaces of afterschool clubs and elective courses to mainstream classes that attract a greater number and wider range of students. To a certain extent, Papert's divide between yearners and schoolers is an artificial one. Most teachers, parents, and students fall somewhere in the middle of these two poles—content with some aspects of schooling and wanting to overhaul other aspects. But for the purpose of more effectively teaching computational thinking and participation in our schools, the binary distinction offers a framework for examining the current methods of teaching computing in K–12 schools, areas where such teaching and learning can improve, and historical models for pedagogical reform.

The first part of this chapter examines the current state of computing education in schools—in both the traditional school classrooms and the less structured learning environments of afterschool programs and DIY initiatives. Where are schoolers and yearners present in each environment, and what is the benefit of each environment for teaching computation on the K–12 level? The second part of the chapter steps away from these two spaces to examine the last time that DIY learning made a widespread entrance into K–12 schools—when the educational theories of John Dewey were new and promised to make school a more practical experience for children. What does this history tell us about yearners' ambitions and schoolers' pragmatism, and what implications can be drawn from the current challenges facing computing education and the integration of technology in schools? This chapter is not intended to be a how-to Scratch guide for teachers. A number of excellent resources, including books and an entire website dedicated to and created by educators, are available for this.[4] Instead, this chapter analyzes the wider culture of schools and the ways that such a culture affects how we teach children how to think and participate computationally.

Computing Education: Inside and Outside of School

According to the U.S. Bureau of Labor Statistics,[5] computing-related jobs are one of the fastest-growing employment fields nationwide. In a country with over 42,000 high schools, however, only 2,100 offer an advanced computer science course. If only 5 percent of this country's high schools offer the advanced computer science courses that prepare students for college classes, then it is clear that computer science has a minimal presence in high schools nationwide, even if their enrollment numbers have been increasing in recent years. This lack of presence is particularly evident in the low numbers of women and minority students who participate in advanced computer science courses at the high school level. Although high school girls are over half of all those who take advanced placement tests, less than a quarter of those who take the computer science test are female, and the number of African American test takers consistently ranks under one percent.[6]

This lack of diversity in students who take advanced high school computing courses reflects curricula and pedagogy that need updating, and over the past two years the College Board has piloted a revised Advanced Placement offering called Computer Science Principles. Courses such as "The Beauty and Joy of Computing"[7] are replacing language-centric courses such "Introduction to Java Script." The CS Principles courses offer a more holistic approach to learning computing by stressing computational concepts rather than prioritizing any single programming language. The CS Principles courses also encourage students to maintain portfolios, work collaboratively, and write reflections about the various project-based assignments. This represents the most promising development in school-based computing instruction in recent years.

More closely akin to the bricolage approach advocated by Sherry Turkle and Seymour Papert (see chapter 2), CS Principles moves away from the traditional top-down approach of amassing content via memorization and instead incorporates performance-based tasks in which students learn the abstract principles behind computation by enacting them through the development of artifacts. Focusing on a specific end-product through an iterative process, the CS Principles pilot represents a true change from instruction that is provided entirely in a single language. Whereas earlier instruction emphasized the development of a discrete skill set, the new CS Principles course is rooted in the design of functional applications, embodying learning in the deliverable (as discussed in chapter 3).

Despite the progress that is being made at the upper level, few students have the opportunity to take these higher-level courses. The recent spike in computer science enrollments demonstrates the presence of a small and committed population of students, but what about the other 99 percent of students in U.S. schools? Where do these students encounter computing instruction during the school day? How do districts incentivize their teachers to teach computer science as a field of study? As it turns out, they offer few incentives. Despite the recent increase in the number of students who take the AP computer science exam and select computer science as an undergraduate major, the number of computing-related courses in this country's K–12 schools has decreased over the past decade. According to a report from the Association of Computing Machinery, C. Wilson, L. A. Sudol, C. Stephenson, and M. Stehlik's *Running on Empty: The Failure to Teach K–12 Computer Science in the Digital Age*,[8] the number of introductory computing-related courses has decreased by 17 percent since 2005. Although student enrollments may be marginally up, the number of courses being offered is down since 2005, and the lack of computational participation in introductory technology-based courses means that few students consider taking CS Principles (even if it is offered at their school) or encounter computer science in their K–12 education.

Some countries, such as Israel, have devised a computer science curricula as a mandated science requirement in their schools, but the United States still treats computer science courses as electives—courses that are taken based on personal interest, akin to joining a band or literary magazine.[9] Treating computer science as an elective rather than a math or science credit may initially seem to present no major issue, but such treatment has serious implications. When districts are asked why computer science courses are not offered at their respective schools, they typically give one of two responses. The first response is that the students are not interested. But such lack of interest usually stems directly from the fact that computer science at that school can be taken only as an elective—not as a course that counts for a math or science credit. With student schedules already overloaded with mandated courses, computer science classes that do not count toward core curricula credit are less likely to attract students, and schools are less inclined to offer them. The second response is that there are few qualified instructors who can teach computer science courses. But because computer science is not considered a core curriculum course, schools of education and state departments of education are reluctant to develop rigorous courses for computer science teaching certification, thus failing to offer a certifiable pathway to develop a qualified body of teachers.

Despite this country's national pride in tech giants such as Apple and Google, the United States is falling behind other countries in computing education on the K–12 level. The United Kingdom recently instituted a national computer science curriculum[10] in which computational thinking figures prominently and is pedagogically tiered through four progressive stages, beginning with elementary applications and basic principles before advancing to the acquisition of languages and systematic problem solving. Since the early 1990s, Israel has mandated a rigorous computer science education program on the K–12 level that is grounded in a curriculum that "emphasizes the foundations of algorithmic thinking" and that teaches "programming as a way to get the computer to carry out an algorithm."[11]

These two countries offer potential models for computer science education beyond supplementary afterschool programs and course electives. They credential such courses as core computing. Google's director of education, Maggie Johnson, cites the exclusion of CS standards from this country's emerging set of Common Core State Standards[12] as a tremendous shortcoming of the national initiative, not only in terms of children's capacity to engage with technology but also in their ability to learn fundamental math and science skills through actual application.[13] Given the prominence of the Common Core State Standards (currently adopted by forty-six states), the initiative represents an unprecedented opportunity for the country to begin to integrate CS education nationally, a cause that Computing in the Core[14] has recognized and continues to advocate.

The results of any such core curriculum are readily apparent. Visitors to any U.S. elementary, middle, or high school, public or private, are unlikely to see any formal teaching related to computer science or to computers as computational, creative devices. As education historian Larry Cuban notes, schools persist in *teaching computers* rather than *teaching with computers*.[15] Focusing on basic functionality and making the devices the ends rather than the means for teaching, technology courses on the K–12 level remain devoid of any real content other than the computers themselves. And although learning the applications of the Microsoft Office suite or familiarizing oneself with the constituent parts of the computer have educational value, such activities do not capture the creative and collaborative potential of computing and do not merit a semester-long course. This lack of robust, introductory computing instruction is at the heart of the nationwide failure of the schoolers. Despite having the machines in the schools for over thirty years, schools have largely failed to enact meaningful change in the way that children think about and participate in using them.

There has been some promise in the peripheral activities that have been occurring at school—but outside of the school day. Afterschool programs have consistently been the places at schools where the most interesting learning with technology has taken place. Whether helping students make video games in a Scratch gamers club, construct collaboratively programmable robots in a Lego Robotics club, or design interactive light-up masks with the Lilypad Arduinio, afterschool clubs historically have had the latitude to allow children to work at their own pace in spaces that are more open and social than traditional classrooms. Thousands of community technology centers across the country also support access to computer activities (such as word processing, email, and Web browsing) in underserved communities. Some, like the Computer Clubhouse, have focused on creative uses of computing where youth are encouraged to work on projects of their own, including the programming of animations, games, and music videos. Scratch was designed to make programming accessible to the media-rich interests of youth.[16]

What is unique about most afterschool clubs and community technology centers is their existence as spaces in which students have an opportunity to make their own projects. As is evident with the revised Advanced Placement computer science course (and the activities described in previous chapters), the capacity to make things with technology sits at the heart of computational thinking and participation. As chapter 2 indicates, making with computers takes learning from the abstract and situates it in the concrete, which then can be shared as currency among wider networks of fellow makers. "We are creatures that need to make," writes founder of *MAKE* magazine Dale Dougherty, quoting poet Frank Bidart.[17] Making is a basic human activity, and in his essay "The Maker Mindset," Dougherty names making as the site of children's most exciting, memorable, and important learning.

Dougherty also laments that this inclination to make is often driven out of children at young ages, as schools—especially as students move up grade levels—increasingly eschew making as a remedial, nonacademic activity. "The biggest challenge and the biggest opportunity for the Maker Movement," Dougherty writes of the DIY community, "is to transform education.... Students are seeking to direct their own education lives, looking to engage in creative and stimulating experiences. Many understand the difference between the pain of education and the pleasure of real learning. Unfortunately, they are forced to seek opportunities outside of school to express themselves and demonstrate what they can do."[18]

Club Meets Class: Searching for the Middle Ground

If it is realistic to expect that the pleasures of the maker culture that surface in afterschool clubs can also exist during the school day, then to some extent the way that schooling is conceived and practiced must fundamentally change. Dale Dougherty is a yearner here, as are many who see digital media and DIY programming as challenges to the traditional teacher-student paradigm of schooling. This is also discussed in "Is New Media Incompatible with Schooling?," media theorist Henry Jenkins's interview with education researcher Richard Halverson, the coauthor (with Allan Collins) of *Rethinking Education in the Age of Technology: The Digital Revolution and Schooling in America*. For Halverson, the future of technology in K–12 schools depends less on the devices themselves and more on various perspectives on how people best learn. According to one perspective, learning happens in schools, and schools are accredited brick-and-mortar spaces. Halverson calls this the "institutional channel." According to another perspective, learning does not have to be linked to time and geography, and Web 2.0 can provide learning opportunities through peer and interest-driven activities. Referring to this as the "digital media channel," Halverson notes that learning in this manner is not standardized and is often unpredictable but that it does "highlight three critically important aspects of learning missing from many school learning activities: motivation, production, and legitimate audience.[19]

Halverson's distinction between the institutional channel and the digital media channel is reminiscent of Papert's distinction between schoolers and yearners. Are students more motivated and productive in afterschool clubs than they are during their regular school classes? Are students more likely to encounter genuine audiences in clubs of their peers than in a classroom? To investigate these questions of motivation, production, and legitimate audience, we designed a study in which middle-school students used Scratch in a school class and in an afterschool club.[20] We wanted to know if there was a difference in how children were motivated in each space, what they produced in each environment, and for whom they produced such content.

Building on Dougherty's notion of students and teachers as makers of a school's learning environment, we constructed two spaces for learning Scratch. One was a language arts class in which middle-school students were introduced to Scratch as a tool for composing their own digital stories in a writing workshop. Class participants followed a scripted curriculum that was tied to statewide academic standards in English language arts. The other group created Scratch projects in an afterschool fan-fiction club. Club participants shared their work, offered feedback to each other, but followed no scripted lessons or submission requirements. The class and the club met for ten consecutive weeks with the same instructor. The class set goals for students, who, by the end of ten weeks, were expected to submit a storyboard of their projected storylines, prepare a digital draft in Scratch, provide peer feedback, hand in a final submission, and make a presentation. The projects were graded, and attendance was mandatory. The club set no goals for participants. They all were encouraged to make a presentation at the end of ten weeks, but no grades were attached, and attendance was not mandated.

Results of this comparison proved interesting. In the class, the deliberate and iterative goals established for the writing workshop played out well in terms of product. Nearly 90 percent of the students completed a digital story, posted it online at the Scratch site, and presented it to their peers at the close of the workshop. Ranging from two to three minutes in length, these stories were based on real-life experiences or cultural icons from movies, television, and comic books. Relatively short but with a clear beginning, middle, and end, these stories included multiple characters and scene changes, and some included dialogue and sound effects. In the club, only 71 percent of the participants completed a project in Scratch, but they produced nearly twice as many projects as those in the class. Projects in the club were also more varied. Although projects in the class setting were all narrative stories, club projects included interactive art pieces and video games, which meant that more types of coding concepts were utilized.

These findings are far from conclusive but suggest that some Scratch after-school club members engaged computationally more than their counterparts in the class did. Although 30 percent of club members never completed or submitted a project, the 70 percent who did submit projects were more fully engaged than their peers in the classroom. Many club members completed four or five projects over the ten-week period. These club members also created richer online profiles at the Scratch site, friended others online, and remixed others' work more often (26 percent of projects were remixed in the club versus 10 percent in the classroom). In the classroom, students twice accused their classmates of cheating by remixing others' work.

Yet the higher completion rate in the classroom (90 percent versus 71 percent in the club) is an argument for integrating computational learning into the school day. And although the classroom students' story-based submissions were more uniform, this uniformity made assessment and assigning a final grade easier. Despite the wishes of some yearners who wish to rid school of grading scales, assessment plays a significant role in ensuring that project-based learning enters classrooms and remains there as part of instruction.

Finally, the 90 percent completion rate in the class was attained in a roomful of students who had not necessarily elected to be in the class (the program was part of their language arts curriculum). The club members had elected to join the afterschool program and show up on a daily basis. Teaching them to use Scratch and engage computationally was in a sense "preaching to the choir." In the class, students who would not necessarily choose to engage in such computing-based learning were exposed to it and engaged with it. The classroom's potential to reach the previously unreachable was captured in the last week of the program when we interviewed participants. We asked Mitch, a seventh-grader who was particularly successful in the classroom environment, whether he also would be interested in the afterschool environment. After a moment of thought, he replied, "I would. But I like sports, too, so I probably wouldn't really fit in."

DIY in the Past and Future: Supporting Learners' Agency

How do teachers make the computational connection for students like Mitch? What is the middle ground between class and club where the best of both environments can be engaged? How does the connected teacher act? These questions are explored by Scratch team member Karen Brennan in her dissertation, "Best of Both Worlds: Issues of Structure and Agency in Computational Creation, in and out of School," where she investigates the relationship between children's learning of Scratch on their own in DIY networks and in the more traditional environment of schools. "Designers of agency-supported learning environment," she writes, "rather than setting structure in opposition to agency, should judiciously employ structure in order to amplify agency."[21]

Five years ago, Brennan could have directed this charge to designers of computational media applications because at that time, there was a push to make tools accessible for children to learn programming.[22] But in this quote, Brennan is referring to teachers. The real challenge today is not to make new and improved tools but to make new and improved classrooms that can incorporate such tools. Young learners need structure, and DIY learning relies on that structure when it gives them the latitude to play with existing rules and guidelines.

Brennan's point here is reminiscent of one of the first DIY advocates in U.S. schools, John Dewey. The classrooms of the University of Chicago

Laboratory Schools, which Dewey founded at the turn of the twentieth century, set them apart from most U.S. classrooms, then and now. There were no desks, and the blackboard (if there was a blackboard) was not the featured wall piece. Students worked at tables facing each other rather than the instructor, and they worked with their hands, not just using pencils and paper but handling actual objects. Engaging in activities that produced content and meaning beyond the classroom—whether boiling an egg or building a wooden box—was an imperative in Dewey's educational philosophy of Progressivism. "If the impulse is exercised, utilized," he writes in *The School and Society*, "it runs up against the actual world of hard conditions to which it must accommodate itself; and there again come in the factors of discipline and knowledge."[23]

For Dewey, the learning activities that schools promote must be applicable and testable in the worlds that children occupy outside of the classroom. Teaching must connect the classroom to the real world. To accomplish this, Dewey points, structure—not the lack of structure—underpins his approach to teaching. Dewey's notion of creating situations and providing materials resonates with Papert's view that saw "teaching without curriculum does not mean spontaneous, free-form classrooms or simply 'leaving the child alone.' It means supporting children as they build their own intellectual structures with materials drawn from the surrounding culture. In this model, educational intervention means changing the culture, planning new constructive elements in it, and eliminating noxious ones."[24] For Papert, the computer provided the materials, situations, and experiences that allow learners to connect to the real world.

For Dewey, experience cannot be simply any experience, and equally, technology cannot be used as an end in itself. "By its nature," Dewey writes in *Experience and Nature*, "technology is concerned with things and acts in their instrumentalities, not in their immediacies."[25] It cannot be assumed that simply having devices in the classroom is enough for children to comprehend their full potential. Dewey also points out that schools nevertheless have an obligation to address the latest technologies. "Technology is modifying, even revolutionizing conduct and belief outside the school," he writes (with J. L. Childs) in 1933: "It is our conviction, accordingly, that … the social and educational theories and conceptions must be developed with definite reference to the needs and issues which mark and divide our domestic, economic, and political life in the generation of which we are part."[26] Schools, Dewey asserts, have a responsibility for developing a child's literacy in terms of reading, writing, and mass media. "The public that is literate in use of linguistic tools," he writes of the growing presence of mass media, "but which is not educated in social information and understanding becomes a ready victim of those who use, for their own private economic and political ends, the public press."[27]

Dewey's warning here is prescient of Douglas Rushkoff's own extended warning in *Program or Be Programmed: Ten Commands for a Digital Age* regarding the limitations of participation in the digital publics of Web 2.0 media.[28] Dewey is referring to newspaper moguls like William Randolph Hearst and not social media sites like Facebook, but the message is clear: a technical understanding of the tool is not enough. People need to understand the contexts in which the tool operates and the contexts that it produces. This represents the essential learning, and such learning requires meaningful experience. Computational thinking and participation do not need to make every child a programmer. But by giving children the capacity to make and share, they give children the opportunity to understand the digital public. This is why programming is not only the new literacy of the millennium but may be the defining literacy of future generations.

Connecting Teaching to Computing

When teachers facilitate technology experiences that are motivating, productive, and socially meaningful, they make room and provide support for children's agency and expression. Robert Taylor's 1980 book, *The Computer in School: Tutor, Tool, Tutee*, offers educators a framework for understanding this scaling capacity of computers. Despite its publication at the beginning of computers' entry into classrooms, Taylor's framing of computers as tutors, tools, and tutees was prescient in designating how students can use computers in the classroom. The computer can be used as a tutor—posting information, asking the learner questions based on such information, and logging and tallying responses for formative, summative, or diagnostic results. As a tool, the computer amplifies communication, such as when Microsoft Powerpoint is used to facilitate a presentation. Finally, as a tutee, the computer serves as the learner by taking directions from the student to determine its function and output.

Taylor's three designations are gradient in nature—that is, not all uses of the computer in school are created equal. The computer as tutor (reminiscent of B. F. Skinner's postwar "teaching machines") has long been under fire in twentieth- and twenty-first-century policy debates over the optimal integration of computers within schools. Placing children in front of interactive screens does not necessarily lead to learning, but the computer as tutor is still relevant. Recently, blended or hybrid learning initiatives have relied heavily on computers in the role of tutors, often relegating teachers to the status of classroom facilitators while students spend most of their time with screens.

The computer as tool may be the most prevalent use of the machine in classrooms today. Teachers selectively use applications to heighten a lecture, distribute a writing assignment, and post feedback to students. The Microsoft Office suite (including Word, Powerpoint, and Excel) is a popular example of using the computer as tool, and most educational research on new classroom literacies centers on using individual programs to integrate computers as teaching and learning tools. New technologies are continuously being made available on the marketplace (Prezi as an alternative to Powerpoint, Google docs as an alternative to Word documents), so many teachable applications highlight the potential of computers as increasingly refined tools. Yet schools need to acknowledge the essential substance that underlines these applications—namely, code. To do this, the classroom will have to graduate to Taylor's third designation—using the computer as tutee. Beaver Country Day School, a small independent school (grades six to twelve) in a Boston suburb, has decided to implement coding across the curriculum, which suggests that some schools are moving on to this third tier.[29] According to the school's profile, Beaver Country Day School was founded and developed on Dewey's Progressive model.[30] And at a nearly $40,000 tuition annually, the school appears to have the resources to implement this ambitious undertaking.

As schools make this jump from using computers as tools to using them as tutees, their most significant resource is their teachers. Computer scientists Andrea Forte and Mark Guzdial have said that, at the introductory school level, computing education should be more about communication than computation.[31] Connected teaching recognizes that students are motivated not by the technology but by the things that they make with the computer and the people with whom they get to share what they make. These ideas are present in Dewey's and Papert's vision of schooling, and this vision is experiencing a renaissance with the growing popularity of maker spaces, DIY learning, and online creative communities where code has become the lingua franca. As the participants in these DIY circles can attest, coding is not just about making the machine compute but also about communicating with the larger world. The divide between yearners and schoolers needs to be bridged to make classrooms more student-centered, product-oriented, and genuinely collaborative. But this divide represents an opportunity in technology education as classrooms and online maker communities offer unique learning environments, which together can increase the number of children who encounter coding as a new literacy and reshape schools' use of computers to be more creative and collaborative. This middle ground— an amalgamation of learning environments—produces the most interesting educational opportunities for children. "It is only in such an ecology of mutations and hybridizations of ways of learning," Papert writes at the close of *The Children's Machine: Rethinking School in the Age of the Computer*, "that a truly new mathetic culture could emerge."[32]

8   Coding for All

On February 26, 2013, the nonprofit organization code.org released a video directed by Lesley Chilcott called "What Schools Don't Teach" on YouTube. The video starts with a quote from Steve Jobs, cofounder of Apple: "Everyone should learn to program a computer ... because it teaches you how to think." And it ends with "One million of the best jobs in America may go unfilled because only one in ten schools teach students how to code." Numerous luminaries speak about their first experiences with getting a computer and writing programs. Bill Gates, cofounder of Microsoft, remembers that he was thirteen when he first got access to a computer and programmed a game that played TicTacToe. Elena Silonek, founder of clothia.com, remembers making a green circle and red square appear on the screen. Gabe Newell, founder of Valve, mentions the sense of wonder he experienced when "Hello, world" came up on the screen for the first time. Mark Zuckerberg, one of Facebook's founders, talks about the process of starting with a simple program and adding to it, and Drew Houston, founder of Dropbox, likens coding to playing an instrument or a sport. Chris Bosh, an All-Star NBA basketball player with the Miami Heat, reflects, "It starts out very intimidating, but you kind of get the hang of it over time. Coding is something that can be learned." The general message of the video is that computers are everywhere. As will.i.am from the rock band The Blackeyed Peas sums up, "Here we are in 2013. All depends on technology—to communicate, to bank, information—and none of us know how to read and write code." The video then calls viewers to action: "Whether you want to be a doctor or a rock star, ask about a coding class at your schools or learn online @ code.org." Within a few days, the video reached millions of viewers. "Bring a little awesomeness to your life," Chilcott urges in a Huffington Post article about the code.org site: "Take a lesson."[1]

A few years earlier, a video in which celebrities discuss their beginnings with computers and programming and urge viewers to learn coding would have been an unlikely success. Yet the excitement and earnestness of those who appear in the YouTube video may be the clearest indication to date that coding is making a comeback. The video showcases three-dimensional animations, music studios, robot drones flying in formation, computer screens in operating rooms, and workplaces with formidable amenities in the software industry. It plays on the sense of empowerment that learning to code can provide individuals. As Valve's founder Gabe Newell's declares, "The programmers of tomorrow are the wizards of the future.... You know, you are going to look like you have magic powers compared to everybody else," and NBA player Chris Bosh adds moments later, "It's amazing.... I think it's the closest thing we have to a super power." Panoramic screen shots of the sleek offices occupied by these programmers tacitly connect learning to code with finding financially rewarding employment and sweeping skyline views.

And yet the February 2013 video also triggers some unease, which education researcher Jane Margolis expresses in March in her closing keynote presentation at the SIGSCE '13 conference for computer science educators. Too often, Margolis points out, the video perpetuates the "boy wonder myth" that programming is more like a superpower rather than a learned skill. It features some women and girls but fails to acknowledge what she categorizes as the "preparatory advantage" that many interviewees had—namely, expensive computers at home in the 1980s, private tutors, and parents who worked in software industry.[2] These key elements are casually referenced by the code.org video's speakers as if they are the rule and not the exception. Access is a significant issue. Before technical prowess can be considered, we need to address some fundamental factors—access to computers, knowledge, and support.

The video focuses on workplaces with open offices and play areas, cafeterias with free snacks, and on-site amenities such as dry cleaning services, but it does not look at the social responsibilities that computer scientists have—to improve onerous working conditions in technology manufacturing, develop better ways to recycle discarded technologies, and increase the participation of underrepresented groups. These issues have received much publicity and suggest that the computer science community needs to reevaluate their public persona. Some, like Vanessa Hirst, the founder of

Girls Develop It, note that "If someone had told me that software is really about humanity, that it is really about helping people by using technology, it would have changed my outlook much earlier."[3] But these alternative, larger-scale perspectives that move coding into the domain of social inter-action and relevance receive little attention in the video, even though this perspective speaks to the day-to-day relevance and civic responsibility of computing.

Finally, although Steve Jobs's introductory quote claims that program-ming "teaches you how to think," programming is only one of many ways to learn computational thinking. Jobs's quote is less grandiose than some others by video interviewees, but it may be both the most powerful and problematic one. If programming is important, then we have a responsi-bility to educate everyone and not suggest that such learning is magic or wizardry. For too long, programming has existed within the popular con-sciousness as an erudite pastime meant for the elite few. The video's prom-ise of superpowers does not do much to change this perception but helps to identify broader issues of access, interest, effort, and support. As long as programming is seen only as a form of thinking and engaging the indi-vidual mind (this is the problematic part) and not equally as a form of par-ticipation and expression (this is the powerful part), we will fail to benefit from learning and teaching code in today's networked communities.

Connected Code: Why Children Need to Learn Programming is a call to action on facilitating computational participation: how do we better design programming activities, tools, and materials for learning and teaching in K–12 schools? We argue that computational thinking should be thought of as computational participation to emphasize that programmed projects like games, stories, and art are not only objects-to-think-with (to use one of Seymour Papert's ideas) but also very much objects-to-share-with that con-nect us to others. Some might argue that bringing programming into K–12 schools will fail now as it failed thirty years ago. Those who persist in seeing programming as a skill meant for the exclusive few also usually persist in seeing it as an inherently asocial activity.

But today, young people participate in computing in websites, clubs, and classrooms, and within this enthusiastic do-it-yourself digital ethic, we see evidence that programming can flourish in schools. This group of young DIY enthusiasts needs to expand so that more children are introduced to the creative and collaborative potential of coding. And Papert's ideas—now over thirty years old—were prescient in terms of understanding that learning to code was most compelling and effective in communal settings. There are sites where millions of kids imagine, design, and freely share their programs. Within the DIY culture, programming is becoming part of the larger digital culture. So as we return programming to the schools, we can draw from lessons learned in the coding circles of Project Headlight and the Scratch online programming community and from a broadened understanding of media practices and repertoire of programmable media.

To expand on Jeanette Wing's definition of computational thinking, we see computational participation as solving problems with others, designing intuitive systems for and with others, and learning about the cultural and social nature of human behavior through the concepts, practices, and perspectives of computer science. Having kids program applications, work in groups, and remix code will not address all of the challenges that are associated with broadening participation in computing, but it represents a crucial beginning step. The commercial toy industry is developing programming applications that allow children to design artifacts that they and others find significant. The popularity of the new maker kits and smart toys illustrates that children want interactive toys that light up and make sounds as well as toys that let them do the interactive designing. They want to determine when the lights blink and the buzzers sound, and educators can foster this spirit in the classroom. By making programming a community effort, educators can make schools into places for sharing and collaboration, both formally and informally.

In the context of computational thinking, this means that we need to move beyond seeing programming as an individualistic act and begin to understand it as a communal practice that reflects how students today can participate in their communities. This is no small step for schools, where individual achievement far outweighs group dynamic in what qualifies for academic success. Yet if the past decade and the advent of Web 2.0 have taught us anything, it is the importance of collaboration in facilitating more creative and cost-effective solutions to problems. Having a chance to participate and collaborate in communities of programming is key to learning the fundamental concepts and practices of programming, which in turn offers people an unprecedented opportunity to participate in the wider digital public.

Focusing on computational participation—as programming activities are returned to schools, community centers, and homes and connected to the online world where many programming projects are designed and shared with others—will be a challenge. Although most schools have not been institutions that support meaningful and productive group work, the magnitude of the challenge is no reason not to rise to meet it. Here we outline multiple pathways that lead to realizing coding for all.

Pathways into Computational Participation

In this book, we have viewed teaching and learning computer coding as being wrapped in theories of mind, community, and culture. According to a good deal of educational research, teaching and learning the three Rs (reading, writing, and arithmetic) need to focus on mind, community, and culture; include skills, strategies, and concepts; and understand context, audience, and relevance. After adding a fourth R for arts (aRts), schools and online and offline afterschool programs will need to add a fifth R for programming (pRogramming).[4] This will involve programming applications for learning specific subject matter, making shareable items with personal meaning, forming communities that provide context and audience for programming designs, leveraging remixing as a cultural practice that children negotiate in appropriate ways, and expanding curriculum to include a broad array of computational materials and activities to generate broad participation in computing. With this in mind, we point to ongoing efforts and new developments that provide promising starting points. Although not an exhaustive list, it serves as a meta-roadmap for new schools, curricula, teachers, afterschool programs, materials, and online communities.

Opportunities need to start in the elementary and middle-school grades to provide students with early experiences in computing. Younger children can engage in creative and constructive designs at home and in kindergarten. Even the iPad, which most children use to play games and watch videos of TV shows, provides an array of simple programming apps (such as Daisy the Dinosaur, Hopscotch, and Move the Turtle) that let kids manipulate objects and characters. A Scratch Jr. version for very young children is being developed based on the original's successful block interface for making designs. But the most interesting advances have been made in the design of tangible construction kits that allow for physical manipulation of blocks to create robots or other devices. Education researcher Marina Bers has provided many compelling examples of how intergenerational robotics workshops can encourage parents and their children to learn together key computational concepts.[5]

In the school setting, ambitious efforts to redesign schools and curricula are integrating programming across the curriculum rather than as a stand-alone class. The instructional software design and game design projects discussed in chapter 3 provide compelling illustrations of how such efforts can be contextualized within an already crowded curriculum rather than offered in a stand-alone course. Similar to the software design projects in Project Headlight in the 1990s, Quest to Learn in New York City (and more recently in Chicago) provides a school environment where students program and play games across the curriculum. With the proliferation of programming tools and communities, there are now numerous examples of game design programs in schools. The nonprofit Globaloria, for example, has created game design classes and competitions in dozens of school districts across several states where students work on designing instructional games in Java, share them with the Globaloria community, and celebrate successes in competitions. Using models such as instructional software design, game design or story telling provide measurably effective ways to integrate computing into standard mathematics and science activities while leveraging students' interest and knowledge of popular digital media.[6]

Equally important are developments of K–12 computer science curricula.[7] The Exploring Computer Science curriculum that was developed by the group around Jane Margolis and Joanna Goode includes a wide range of activities such as interface design, computing and data analysis, and Web and robotics design. Through these activities, students are introduced to problem solving and design thinking as they learn basic programming ideas and concepts and address social issues and the ethics of computing. The curriculum has been successfully implemented in several high schools in the Los Angeles area and is being expanded to schools in cities across the United States. The Association for Computing Machinery and the Computer Science Teachers Association also proposed a model curriculum for K–12 education that included examples of media computing, computing in biology, and computational thinking. Another development is the recent startup of six new computer science and engineering public high schools in New York City with the goal of increasing the number of schools in coming years. The Software Engineering Pilot curriculum takes an equally sweeping approach to introducing fundamental software design and engineering principles in the context of Web design, robotics, and embedded electronics in textile designs, and it complements them with electives in computer-aided design, three-dimensional computer graphics, animation, and bioinformatics. Many schools (such as High Tech High) have promoted a broad spectrum of technology and coding activities in their curricula. These curriculum designs illustrate that computing at the high school level can introduce students to key ideas of computational thinking and create pathways into Advanced Placement computer science courses and exams that present crucial preparation for moving into computer science courses at the college level.

We also need teachers who can implement these curricula and counselors who steer students into courses. After reviewing the situation in Cameron Wilson, Leigh Ann Sudol, Chris Stephenson, and Mark Stehlik's recent report, *Running on Empty: The Failure to Teach K–12 Computer Science in the Digital Age*, the Computer Science Teachers Association has recommended adapting certification standards for teachers. CS cannot be taught by a transient corps of volunteers but will need to include professionals who understand the learning trajectories of students and who develop pedagogical strategies to support learning. We have provided several examples of how computing can be incorporated in the curriculum rather than exist as a stand-alone activity. But as Jane Margolis's work has shown, teachers, administrators, and school counselors all play critical roles in overcoming students' narrow informal conceptions of computing and encouraging them to take available courses.

Although the shift toward designing authentic applications is an important step in the right direction, designing video games is not the only application that can achieve this goal. Game design leverages the interest and informal experiences of many children and youth, but it also caters to a community that is still predominantly male. Many other types of software applications can be designed and fulfill the premise of an authentic context. For this reason, joining the existing clubhouse that might be found in the Scratch community still leaves many outside. In the Scratch online community, only 37 percent of members are girls—more than at many other technical sites but not enough.

To broaden computational participation, we need to encourage all kinds of digital designs, including games, animations, and stories with different materials and contexts. The Alice programming language, for example, has imported Sims characters into its environment to connect students' experiences with entertainment software to programming 3D stories. This inclusion helps promote the site by leveraging popular culture but also tacitly breaks from the traditional "move and shoot" video game motif by encouraging broader interactivity through character development and extended narratives. Equally important are efforts in pedagogy, such as the Programmers' Workshop that built on the established model of the Writers' Workshop to offer teachers and students a structure for including computational activities in digital stories and animation.

Electronic tangible construction kits are making new computing activities available that expand beyond the already popular robotics activities. LilyPad Arduino, MaKey MaKey, and many other kits and materials suggest rich contexts for computing and can lead to computational activities that move beyond the screen into arts and humanities.[8] This is especially important in K–12 classrooms, where early programming activities occurred exclusively in mathematics and science classes. As social sciences, humanities, and media arts evolve in the digital age, these construction kits represent the new "stuff" of teaching and learning. By broadening activities, practices, and perceptions of computing, computational participation can be ensured for all students. Now that technologies have become more widely distributed and more affordable, it is time to develop and promote materials that jump the traditional gender divide that has been associated with robotics. We can no longer be content with youth online communities that simply socialize. Computational participation means connecting through making, which leads to deeper, richer, and healthier connections among online youth.

Although schools, curricula and materials, and teachers are important milestones on this road map, afterschool programs and online communities are equally important in providing access to support, expertise, and audience. The Computer Clubhouse network is a key example of how community technology centers can be more than just places for doing homework and playing games and can engage youth in learning programming. Other community efforts such as GirlsWhoCode.org have focused on girls. The Computer Clubhouse set up successful Girls Days in their centers to create spaces for girls to visit and investigate. Many public libraries have started maker spaces and activities in their branches that often reach underserved communities where they live. These physical locations are important "homes away from home" for many youth to find receptive audiences for their designs.[9]

We also need to figure out ways that youth can participate in online creative communities such as Scratch that allow them to program outside of schools. These online communities provide new models for collaborative action and participation that move far beyond the current model of small-group collaboration that is practiced in many school settings. We have demonstrated how such collaborative activities can be designed and what it means for students to develop collaborative agency. Such collaboration provides authentic extensions to the world outside of school, and as those boundaries around what happens inside and outside classrooms become more fluid, students and teachers connect and share in ways that create healthy and effective learning organizations.

There are many reasons for making these efforts, but they all have one overarching goal: to achieve equity and diversity because computational participation cannot be achieved if only a select few join the clubhouse. After twenty years of only marginal success in broadening participation in computing, we know that this does not happen on its own, just as we know that technology education in K–12 schools does not naturally evolve. It takes real pushing. And we know from our research in the Scratch community that this move toward membership in a large-scale community is a complex interplay between how young software designers develop personal agency through programming and how they gain status as experts among their peers. Despite the myth of children as "digital natives" who naturally migrate online, observations indicate that some children initially resist uploading their program to the Scratch website and are uncomfortable sharing their work with more experienced members online. This suggests that establishing membership in a large programming community is not easily achieved. Navigating online communities requires an array of participation strategies that address the vulnerability that is associated with sharing one's work for others to comment on and even remix for their own purposes.[10]

Likewise, seeing programming as a collaborative, distributed effort requires types of collaborative agency that usually are not found in the collaborative group work in classrooms. In the Scratch online community, for example, collaborative activities typically revolve around the production of particular types of Scratch projects by a small group of individuals who have met one another in the online environment based on mutual interests. In our recent research into such forms of collaborative efforts with online and offline groups, we found that many students found it difficult to participate in these types of self-organized collaboratives. Educators and researchers who design and study K–12 programming communities need to focus not just on how novice students learn to program but also on how children learn to collaborate.

This issue of equity in participation is not new. On a basic level, the classrooms that use software design activities always form communities where students engage in the forms of peer pedagogy that often are observed in large online networks. What is different now is the availability of large-scale communities that connect thousands of young programmers and provide different contexts and opportunities for exchange. The type of design communities that are created around tools such as Scratch, Alice, or Kodu can be done in local classrooms and clubs where youth participate as well as in the online spaces that youth populate to share their designs and comment on others.

These new directions for the design of activities, tools, and communities in K–12 educational computing efforts can broaden participation in and perceptions of computing on a considerably larger scale than previous attempts of integration. We are not arguing that all the standard staples of traditional computing courses should be dismissed. Writing code to learn about the nature of algorithms and developing data structures, compilers, and general architecture remain crucially important and are not easily learned on their own. But K–12 educational computing can take the road that K–12 language arts, mathematics, and science education took long ago. It can successfully leverage the insights that are gained from youth digital media, networked cultures, and learning theory to promote the idea of children programmers against all conventional wisdom.

Coding Is Connecting

We argue that computational thinking should be reframed as computational participation because computers in any form and place have become an inextricable part of our social life by affecting how we interact with each other and how we contribute to our communities. Being today's digital native involves browsing the Web, using technology to communicate, participating in gaming networks, knowing how things are made, contributing through making, and understanding the social and ethical ramifications of our actions. Digital technologies are embedded in the way we live, work, play, socialize, learn, and teach.[11] We not only participate in but also make the digital world that we live in, and this requires understanding the personal, social, cultural, and tangible connections to code.

We no longer need to build a gigantic Walk-Through Computer to connect with the machine because the machine itself now walks with us. As Sherry Turkle argues, computers have already become "the architect of our intimacies."[12] Digital technologies—whether Facebook photos, Twitter feeds, or videos posted on YouTube—represent extensions of ourselves and are a way to emote, ponder, and connect. Architects and city planners realized long ago that citizens need to have a voice in urban planning if cities are to be livable places.[13] Now computer scientists and educators must realize that citizens need to have a voice in computational participation to make the digital publics a livable space, and this, for Jane Margolis, makes computational participation "the civil rights issue of the 21st century."[14]

Although few of us will become computer scientists who write the code and design the systems that undergird our daily life, we all need to understand code to be able to examine digital designs and decisions constructively, creatively, and critically.[15] We are all users of digital technologies for functional, political, and personal purposes. On a functional level, a basic understanding of code allows people to understand the design and functionalities that underlie the interfaces, technologies, and systems that we encounter daily. On a political level, understanding code empowers people and provides resources for examining and questioning the design decisions that populate our screens. Finally, on a personal level, everyone needs code for expressive purposes to communicate and interact with others and build relationships. We need to be able to examine designs and the decisions that went into making them.[16] To capture these multiple purposes of literacy, education activist Paulo Freire said that "reading the word is reading the world." We see reading the code is as much about reading the world as it is about understanding, changing, and remaking the digital world in which we live.

Seymour Papert envisioned the computer as a protean machine, a universal device to construct objects-to-think-with in intellectually rich, personally meaningful, culturally diverse and socially connected ways. In our vision, it is this fourth component—connectivity—that emerges as crucial if children are to learn computing as a fundamental skill. Objects-to-share-with represent the new imperative and new standard when it comes to learning and making with digital media. It is here, in the moment of exchange, that the computer may deliver on its protean promise for connecting in a networked world.

Notes

Chapter 1

1. For more information on the Walk-Through Computer, see the press kit at http://research.microsoft.com/enus/um/people/gbell/tcmwebpage/WalkThrougPressKit.pdf and the video at http://www.youtube.com/watch?v=CoxQLJkLq1c. General information about the history and exhibits in The Computer Museum can be found at http://en.wikipedia.org/wiki/The_Computer_Museum,_Boston. The archive about the history of computing was moved to the Tech Museum of Innovation (http://www.thetech.org) in San Jose, California.

2. Stewart Brand's 1988 book *The Media Lab: Inventing the Future* includes a chapter on Project Headlight's early days. In addition, several dissertations and books detail many of the projects that took place at Project Headlight, among them Idit Harel's *Children Designers: Interdisciplinary Constructions for Learning and Knowing Mathematics in a Computer-Rich School* (1991), Yasmin Kafai's *Minds in Play: Computer Game Design as a Context for Children's Learning* (1995), Michele Evard's *Twenty Heads are Better Than One: Communities of Children as Virtual Experts* (1998), and Ricki Goldman-Segall's *Points of Viewing of Children's Thinking: Digital Ethnographer's Journey* (1998.

3. This is a theme that Sherry Turkle examines in *Second Self: Computers and the Human Spirit* (1984), in *Life on the Screen: Identity in the Age of the Internet* (1995), and most recently in *Alone Together: Why We Expect More from Technology and Less from Each Other* (2011).

4. The short video *What Most Schools Don't Teach* was directed by Lesley Chilcott, produced by code.org, released on YouTube on February 26, 2013, and reached over 10 million views within the first three weeks of its posting. Earlier work such as Andrea DiSessa's *Changing Minds: Computers, Learning, and Literacy* (2001), Marc Prensky's "Programming Is the New Literacy" (2008), and Douglas Rushkoff's *Program or Be Programmed: Ten Commands for a Digital Age* (2010) have made similar arguments for learning programming.

5. Computational thinking was introduced in an essay published by Jeanette Wing in 2006 and expanded in 2010. The increasing popularity of computational thinking spurred the foundation of a research center at Carnegie Mellon University (http://www.cs.cmu.edu/~CompThink).

6. For reports on youth' digital media use, see The Kaiser Family Foundation's *Generation M²: Media in the Lives of Eight- to Eighteen-Year-Olds* (Rideout, Foehr, and Roberts 2010) and M. Ito et al.'s *Hanging Out, Messing Around, and Geeking Out: Living and Learning with New Media* (2009). For more details on the nature and dynamics of participation in social networks, see Yochai Benkler's *The Wealth of Networks: How Social Production Transforms Markets and Freedom* (2006), and on the DIY movement, see David Gauntlett's *Making Is Connecting: The Social Meaning of Creativity from DIY and Knitting to YouTube and Web 2.0* (2011), Mark Frauenfelder's *Made by Hand: Searching for Meaning in a Throwaway World* (2011), and Chris Anderson's *Makers: The New Industrial Revolution* (2012).

7. See Wing (2006, 6).

8. Two reports on the National Research Council's workshops (2010, 2011) present definitions, applications, and pedagogical approaches. A 2013 article by Shoshi Grover and Roy Pea in the *Educational Researcher* reviews several approaches to defining computational thinking but did not include the operational definition by Karen Brennan and Mitchel Resnick (2012) that we are using in this book.

9. See http://www.google.com/edu/computational-thinking.

10. For more information, consult the list of resources at the end of the book.

11. The framework of computational concepts, practices, and perspectives was developed by Karen Brennan and Mitchel Resnick (2012) to articulate different aspects of computational thinking.

12. For one of the first reports examining issues of equity and diversity around technology in schools, see Rosemary Sutton (1991). Beth McGrath Cohoon and William Asprey (2006) and Mark Warschauer and T. Matuchniak (2010) present a more recent review. Numerous other publications have addressed these issues, in particular Jane Margolis and Allan Fisher's *Unlocking the Clubhouse: Women in Computing* (2002) and Margolis et al.'s *Stuck in the Shallow End: Education, Race, and Computing* (2008).

13. In *Confronting the Challenges of Participation Culture*, Henry Jenkins et al. (2006) introduce the concept of participation gap to emphasize access to participation. This was in contrast to work on the digital divide that emphasized access to hardware and networks (see Sutton 1991).

14. College Board (2012).

15. Bureau of Labor Statistics (2012).

16. *Developing a Media-Rich Programming Environment*, funded by a 2003 National Science Foundation grant to Mitchel Resnick, Natalie Rusk, John Maloney, and Yasmin Kafai (NSF 0325828), supported the initial development of Scratch. *Preparing the Next Generation of Computational Thinkers*, funded by a 2010 NSF grant to Mitchel Resnick, Yasmin Kafai, and Yochai Benkler (NSF 1027848/1027736/1026473), focuses on the relationship between computation and collaboration.

17. See Yasmin Kafai, Kylie Peppler, and Robbin Chapman, *The Computer Clubhouse: Creativity and Constructionism in Youth Communities* (2009), for more details on the design and evaluation of activities.

18. Henry Jenkins provides an overview on the new directions in DIY, youth media, and learning in an afterword to Michele Knobel and Colin Lankshear's *DIY Media: Creating, Sharing, and Learning with New Technologies* (2010), but see also the books by A. Spencer (2005) and Barbara Guzetti, K. Elliot, and D. Welsch (2010).

Chapter 2

1. See Seymour Papert (1993b, preface, "The Gears of My Childhood").

2. Early references to the term of *connected learning* can be found in Seymour Papert's 1996 book *The Connected Family: Bridging the Digital Generation Gap* and in Uriel Wilensky's Center for Connected Learning at Northwestern University (http://ccl .northwestern.edu), started in 1995, which described its mission as enabling "learners to make deep connections between what they are learning and their personal experience of the world." The 2013 report *Connected Learning: An Agenda for Research and Design* by Mizuko Ito and colleagues does not explicitly refer to these earlier efforts but embodies many of the same ideas.

3. Papert worked in Jean Piaget's research group in Geneva between 1958 and 1963 and incorporated main tenets of Piaget's genetic epistemology in his development of constructionist theory (see Papert 1991).

4. See Sherry Turkle (2007).

5. Logo was initially developed by the late Wally Feurzeig and his research group at Bolt, Beranek, and Newman (BBN), which hired Seymour Papert as a consultant. For more information on the development of Logo, particularly its initial conception, see Feurzeig (2010).

6. The development of microworlds that incorporate parallel programming versions was conceptualized in NetLogo by Uriel Wilensky and in StarLogo by Mitchel Resnick (1991). Programming applications were used to illuminate natural phenomena, and human phenomena can be described this way, as Mitchel Resnick and Uriel Wilensky (1998) have pointed out. Papert defined *microworld* as "a computer-based interactive learning environment where the prerequisites are built into the system

and where learners can become the active, constructing architects of their own learning" (Papert 1993b, 122). A wide range of microworlds in mathematics and science has been developed since then, and not all of them are Logo-based environments. For more examples of microworlds and further developments see A. diSessa (2000), L. Edwards (1998), and Richard Noss and Celia Hoyles (1996).

7. These claims did not remain uncontested. Much has been written about the success or failure of Logo in schools, but it is worth providing some background to the debate. In an excellent analysis of the historical context in the United States and in Europe, Richard Noss and Celia Hoyles (1996) identify some of the cultural forces at play that led critics to ask certain questions about Logo and not others. In many schools, questions about Logo's learning benefits focused on the transfer of problem-solving skills and not on the benefits of learning mathematics and pedagogical reform ideas. Several smaller studies conducted by Roy Pea and Midian Kurland (1984) are often referenced as evidence that learning Logo programming did not produce any transferable effects. These studies neglected aspects of learning such as length of time spent learning programming and the types of programs created. These features have now been recognized as being instrumental in designing successful programming instruction (Palumbo 1990) and are discussed in more detail in chapter 3. In addition, teachers often adopted Logo but not the pedagogical innovations, and when they did adopt the innovations, many did not receive widespread institutional support in their schools. Many institutional forces shaped the use and success of Logo in schools, but the pedagogical ideas about learning and teaching were often the least acknowledged.

8. For more detail on the role that is played by informal knowledge in learning, see J. Bransford, A. Brown, and R. Cocking (2000); for the role played by cultural knowledge, see N. Gonzáles, L. Moll, and C. Amanti (2005); and for the need to combine both, see A. Sfard (1998).

9. Papert (1993a, 105).

10. For more detail, see the seminal work of Jeanne Lave and Etienne Wenger (1991) on apprenticeship culture and the work on affinity groups by Jim Gee (2003). Y. B. Kafai, W. Burke, and C. Mote (2012) and Kafai, K. Searle, E. Kaplan, D. Fields, E. Lee, and D. Lui (2012) have focused on collaborative agency, which builds on M. Scardamalia's (2002, 2) collaborative collective responsibility to explain students' achievements in learning to understand the "conditions in which responsibility for the success for a group is distributed across all the members rather than being concentrated on the leader."

11. Papert (1993b, 178).

12. For more information on the Computer Clubhouse, see Y. Kafai, K. A. Peppler, and R. Chapman (2009), and see also the article by J. P. Zagal and A. Bruckman (2005) on the learning cultures of Brazilian samba school. MOOSE Crossing is

described in A. Bruckman (1997), more information on the development of the ClubZora community can be found in M. Bers (2012), and the research on online creative collaboration in the Newgrounds community can be found K. Luther, K. Caine, K. Ziegler, and A. Bruckman (2010).

13. See Sherry Turkle and Seymour Papert (1991). Another example highlights cultural preferences for understanding phenomena such as bee hives and traffic jams. We often assume causal relationships when in fact these are complex systems whose behaviors emerge out of the interactions among smaller simpler actions. M. Resnick and U. Wilensky (1998) called such thinking the centralized mindset that assumes that a central agent such as the queen bee is responsible for coordinating the activities of bees.

14. For a more extended discussion of critical making and citizenship, see the upcoming book by Matt Ratto and Megan Boler (2014). For a more extended discussion of the revaluation of the concrete in academic learning, see Uri Wilensky (1991).

15. Papert (1993b, 63–68).

16. Turkle and Papert (1991, 4). But for more detail on the Lego/Logo construction kits, see Resnick and Ocko (1991) and also F. Martin (1996, 2001).

17. Kelleher and Pausch (2005, 132).

18. "Does wood produce good houses? If I built a house out of wood and it fell down, would this show that wood does not produce good houses? Do hammers and saws produce good furniture? These questions betray themselves as technocentric questions by ignoring people and elements that only people can introduce: skill, design, and aesthetics" (Papert 1980, 24).

Chapter 3

1. Idit Harel, *Children Designers: Interdisciplinary Construction for Learning and Knowing Mathematics in a Computer-Rich School* (1991, xv–xvi).

2. See the work by Leen Streefland (1991) and others in mathematics education.

3. For more on the instructional software design project, see Idit Harel and Seymour Papert (1990) and Harel (1991).

4. For more comprehensive overviews on research on learning programming, see D. Clements (1999), Clements and J. S. Meredith (1993), Clements and J. Sarama (1997), A. Robbins, J. Rountree, and N. Rountree (2003), and E. Soloway and J. Spohrer (1990).

5. Research by R. D. Pea and D. M. Kurland (1983) raised critical points about the absence of planning and problem solving in learning programming Logo. But see

also C. Holyes and R. Noss (1990) for a discussion on the study design and a historical perspective on the debate.

6. C. Salomon and D. N. Perkins (1987).

7. David Palumbo (1990).

8. J. Lave (1988), Lave and E. Wenger (1991), J. S. Brown, A. Collins, and P. Duguid (1989). For a more comprehensive overview, see J. Bransford, A. Brown, and R. Cocking (2000).

9. David Shaffer and Mitchel Resnick (1999) identify these different meanings of authenticity in a literature review. The focus on funds of knowledge has been promoted by N. González, L. Moll, and C. Amanti (2005).

10. This work was inspired by the idea of "design for learning" (Perkins 1986), *The Sciences of the Artificial* (Simon 1981), and *The Reflective Practitioner: How Professionals Think in Action* (Schön 1983), which had just gained traction in the education community. Professional practices in design disciplines were seen as contexts that promote open-ended forms of problem solving and situated learners in the application of academic content in the design of meaningful, authentic applications.

11. Tim O'Reilly (2005) coined the term *Web 2.0* in his article "What Is Web 2.0?" Others, such as Marc Prensky (2008) and Doug Rushkoff (2010), also have promoted the design of applications as a way to engage digital natives in better understanding digital media.

12. Papert (1993, 109).

13. Papert (1991, 111).

14. A. Collins and R. Halverson (2009).

15. This was done by initiating and expanding science conversations in groups (Kafai and Ching 2001), by helping younger inexperienced teams with planning their instructional designs (Marshall 2000), and by providing programming assistance when needed (Ching and Kafai 2008). Perceptions of software designers also change over time (Kafai and Roberts 2002), as was found in one of the few longitudinal examinations of long-term programming learning.

16. J. Gee (2003) and K. Squire (2011).

17. Y. B. Kafai (1995); see also Kafai (1996, 1998).

18. J. Cassell and H. Jenkins (1998).

19. See J. Denner and S. Campe (2008), C. Heeter and B. Winn (2008), C. Pelletier (2008), E. R. Hayes and I. A. Games (2008), and K. A. Peppler and Y. B. Kafai (2007). For a general overview on the underrepresentation of women in IT, see Cohoon and Asprey (2006). For the situation in the gaming industry, see Y. B. Kafai, C. Heeter, J. Denner, and J. Y. Sun (2008).

20. Alice by C. Kelleher (2008) and Scratch by M. Resnick et al. (2009).

21. L. Resnick (1987).

22. B. Feinberg (2007).

23. L. Calkins (1986).

24. Q. Burke and Y. B. Kafai (2012).

25. D. Dougherty (2010).

26. For more examples of writing, see Q. Burke (2012); for more examples in science, see C. C. Ching and Y. B. Kafai (2008); and for applications to music, see G. Gargarian (1996).

27. The descriptions and analysis of Computer Clubhouse activities, mentor support, and Scratch projects are drawn from reports in Y. Kafai, K. A. Peppler, and R. Chapman (2009). The case study of Jorge can be found in Peppler and Kafai (2007). There is a small but growing body of work that has studied youth practices in schools, afterschool clubs and community technology centers.

28. See Kafai and Peppler (2007).

29. More detail on Jorge's case study can be found in Kafai and Peppler (2007).

30. See Ito et al. (2009) for a general overview on youth's engagement with digital media, Rebecca Black's (2008) work on fan fiction and Barbara Guzetti and Margaret Gamboa (2004) on zine culture.

31. D. Wolber, H. Abelson, E. Spertus, and L. Looney (2011).

32. M. Resnick and B. Silverman (2005).

33. Burke and Kafai (2012, 131).

Chapter 4

1. For more on the BBC online report, see J. Fildes (2007). Andrés Monroy-Hernández's 2012 dissertation, "Designing for Remixing: Supporting an Online Community of Amateur Creators," provides a detailed account of the beginnings of the Scratch online site. The research on Green Bear Productions is also documented in C. Aragon, S. Poon, and A. Monroy-Hernández (2009) and at the History page at http://graybear.webs.com.

2. Books by Y. Benkler (2006) and E. von Hippel (2005) discuss Web 2.0 trends.

3. Seymour Papert (1975).

4. T. DeMarco and T. Lister (1999).

5. See the footage at code.org.

6. For a full overview of different Logo versions, see the compilation at http://elica. net/download/papers/LogoTreeProject.pdf.

7. Alan Kay and Adele Goldberg (1977).

8. Andrea diSessa (2001) sees coding less as a "hard" technical application of math and science and more as a "literacy" that allows all individuals to create digital content and refine their thinking.

9. Mark Guzdial (2004a, 2004b).

10. S. Holloway and G. Valentine (2003).

11. Caitlin Kelleher and Randy Pausch (2005, 132).

12. See Jane Margolis and Allan Fisher, *Unlocking the Clubhouse: Women in Computing* (2002), which focuses on the gender divide in computing, and Jane Margolis, R. Estrella, J. Goode, J. J. Holme, and K. Nao, *Stuck in the Shallow End: Education, Race, and Computing* (2008), which addresses the steep socioeconomic and racial gaps in children's use of technology in schools.

13. Mitchel Resnick and Brian Silverman (2005).

14. See A. Repenning and A. Ioannidou (2008), K. J. Harms et al. (2012), and A. Games (2012).

15. J. Lave and E. Wenger (1991) and E. Wenger (2004).

16. J. Gee (2003).

17. For more information, see S. Fox and M. Madden (2006), Yochai Benkler's 2006 *The Wealth of Networks: How Social Production Transform Markets and Freedom* (2006), and Clay Shirky's *Cognitive Surplus: Creativity and Generosity in the Connected Age* (2010).

18. N. Webb (1980).

19. Laurie Williams et al. (2000).

20. Extensive research on pair programming has been conducted by D. Denner and L. Werner (2007) and G. Braught, L. M. Eby, and T. Wahls (2008).

21. Amy Bruckman (1997).

22. Ibid., 184.

23. For more on the role of MOOSE Crossing's influence on the Scratch website, see Andrés Monroy-Hernández's dissertation (2012, chap. 2).

24. Ibid., 77.

25. Y. Kafai, K. A. Peppler, and R. Chapman (2009).

26. See Scratch community analytics, which are updated monthly at http://stats .scratch.mit.edu/community.

27. A. Monroy-Hernández and M. Resnick (2008).

28. Monroy-Hernández (2012, 38).

29. Harms et al. (2012).

30. Y. B. Kafai, D. A. Fields, R. Roque, W. Q. Burke, A. Monroy-Hernández (2012).

31. See K. Brennan, A. Monroy-Hernández, and M. Resnick's 2010 "Making Projects, Making Friends: Online Communities as Catalysts for Interactive Media Creation" as a microcosm of this level of connectivity as it anecdotally exists in Scratch. See also David Gauntlett's 2011 *Making Is Connecting: The Social Meaning of Creativity from DIY and Knitting to YouTube and Web 2.0* for a wider treatment of the growing relationship between productivity and interconnectivity, creativity and collaboration.

32. For more interviews with members of the online community, see Karen Brennan's dissertation (2012, 114).

33. Ibid., 213.

34. A. Monroy-Hernández and B. Mako Hill (2010).

35. See http://wiki.scratch.mit.edu/wiki/Scratch_Wiki.

36. Kurt Luther and Amy Bruckman (2011).

37. Brennan (2012, 109–110).

38. Ibid., 107.

39. Aragon, Poon, and Monroy-Hernández (2009).

40. For more on modularization and the nature of information hiding in programmed systems, see D. Parnas's (1972) influential paper "On the Criteria to Be Used in Decomposing Systems Into Modules," http://www.cs.umd.edu/class/ spring2003/cmsc838p/Design/criteria.pdf.

41. Monroy-Hernández (2012).

42. R. Roque (2012).

43. K. Luther, K. Caine, K. Ziegler, and A. Bruckman (2011).

44. D. A. Fields, M. Giang, and Y. B. Kafai (2013).

45. See M. Thomas's 2011 book *Deconstructing Digital Natives: Young People, Technology, and the New Literacies* for a reconsideration of the term that Marc Prensky coined in 2001.

46. See Y. B. Kafai, D. A. Fields, and W. Q. Burke (2010).

47. For more on the nature of the Lorenz curve as applied to economic inequality, see J. L. Gastwirth's 1972 "The Estimation of the Lorenz Curve and Gini Index."

48. Brennan (2013, 118–120).

49. See the initial Collab Challenge at http://info.scratch.mit.edu/collabchallenge.

50. See Kafai, Fields, Roque, Burke, and Monroy-Hernández (2012).

51. Ibid., 72.

52. Luther, Caine, Ziegler, and Bruckman (2011).

53. A. Lenhart (2007).

54. Y. B. Kafai, W. Burke, and C. Mote (2012); Kafai, K. Searle, E. Kaplan, D. Fields, E. Lee, and D. Lui 2012).

55. J. Zhang, M. Scardamalia, R. Reeve, and R. Messina (2009).

56. Alicia M. Magnifico (2010).

57. Harms et al. (2012).

58. R. Reynolds and M. Chiu (2013).

59. M. Resnick (2012).

Chapter 5

1. Public tournaments were organized around these competitions, with hundreds of onlookers following every move of the ball, their heads darting back and forth from paddle to paddle. It was infectious game play and became the model for digital gaming as we know it. For more, see M. Wolf (2008) and David Winter (1996).

2. A. Monroy-Hernández, B. Mako Hill, J. Gonzalez-Rivero, and d. boyd (2011, 81).

3. See S. Jayadevappa and R. Shankar (2009) for further details on how the nature of teaching programming has changed.

4. For an excellent and brief overview of remix, see C. Lankshear and M. Knobel (2008). For an in-depth examination of the concept, see D. Goldberg (2004).

5. Y. Benkler (2006); Clay Shirky (2010).

6. D. A. Fields, M. Giang, and Y. B. Kafai (2013).

7. A. Bader-Natal, A. Monroy-Hernández, J. D. Zamfirescu-Pereira, and S. Farnham (2012).

8. For a copy, go to http://creativecommons.org/licenses/by-sa/3.0.

9. For the Scratch Community Guidelines, see http://scratch.mit.edu/community _ guidelines.

10. Monroy-Hernández et al. (2011).

11. Ibid.

12. K. Brennan, A. Monroy-Hernández, and M. Resnick (2010).

13. For more on the nature of communities of practice and their role in facilitating shared enterprise, see J. Lave and E. Wenger (1991).

14. David Parnas (1972).

15. K. Brennan (2012, 75).

16. Seymour Papert (2002).

17. J. V. Nickerson and A. Monroy-Hernández (2012).

18. Giorgos Cheliotis and Jude Yew (2009).

19. For a more detailed examination of the various past collaborative challenges and camps, see R. Roque (2012).

20. A. Collins and R. Halverson (2009).

21. S. M. Williams (2009).

22. Lanksher and Knobel (2008); L. Manovich (2005).

23. For an overview, see K. A. Mills (2010).

24. B. Mako Hill, A. Monroy-Hernández, and K. Olson (2010).

25. Y. B. Kafai, D. A. Fields, and W. Q. Burke (2010).

26. L. Lessig (2008).

27. B. Mako Hill and A. Monroy-Hernández (2013).

28. For more information on the GoodPlay project, see James et al. (2009) or visit their website http://www.pz.gse.harvard.edu/good_play.php.

29. Sherry Turkle and Seymour Papert (1991, 165).

30. Y. B. Kafai (1995, 70).

31. Betsy DiSalvo et al. (2009)

32. J. Griffin, E. Kaplan, Q. Burke, and Y. B. Kafai (2010).

33. John Maloney et al. (2004, 107).

34. Vito Campanelli (2012, 11).

35. P. Thagard (2012).

36. For more on this notion of software as information, see M. C. Jones (2010, chap. 2).

Chapter 6

1. For a more detailed description of the design and development of MaKey MaKey, see Jay Silver, Eric Rosenbaum, and David Shaw (2012). See Makey Makey's page at Kickstarter at http://www.kickstarter.com/projects/joylabs/makey-makey-an-inven tion-kit-for-everyone. For an overview of funded Kickstarter campaigns, see http:// www.kickstarter.com/discover/categories/technology/most-funded.

2. See http://robotics-africa.org.

3. See http://arduino.org and http://arduino.cc for two examples of such communi- ties. Several books have captured different aspects of the maker and DIY movements. See Neil Gershenfeld's *Fab: The Coming Revolution on Your Desktop—From Personal Computers to Personal Fabrication* (2007), for an introduction to the fabrication labo- ratory (fablab) idea, Chris Anderson's *Makers: The New Industrial Revolution* (2012) for a business perspective, Mark Frauenfelder's *Made by Hand: Searching for Meaning in a Throwaway World* (2010) (which describes DIY efforts at home), and David Gaunt- lett's *Making Is Connecting: The Social Meaning of Creativity from DIY and Knitting to YouTube and Web 2.0* (2011), pointing to prior movements such as the fanzine culture.

4. See a 2013 chapter by Dale Dougherty, founder of *Make* Magazine, where he out- lines the main directions of the maker movement.

5. An early article by Mike Eisenberg and Ann Eisenberg (1998) projected a new type of shop class for schools. Margaret Honey and David Canter (2013) compiled various efforts in science centers and museums, and B. Barron, K. Gomez, N. Pinkard, and C. K. Martin (2014) illustrate implementations in afterschool and library programs. For developments in the Boy Scouts, see Kathryn Dillis's "Game Design Badge: Boy Scouts Embrace the Digital World" (2013).

6. For an image, go to http://www.wired.com/geekdad/2007/03/the_origins_of_.

7. The first writings about Lego/Logo were by Mitchel Resnick and Steven Ocko (1991), but see also Resnick (1993), Resnick, Fred Martin, Randy Sargent, and B. Sil- verman (1996) and Martin (1996).

8. Lego/Logo was called Lego TC Logo in 1988. A later generation of the technology became Lego Mindstorms, which was launched in 1998.

9. For more information on the history of autonomous robots competitions, see http://spacecats.mit.edu/about/history.shtml. It is widely believed that these kinds

of public activities, where students prepare, display, and share their learning artifacts, can be valuable learning experiences, yet few researchers have studied what students derive from their participation in science fairs and robotics competitions. S. Yasar and D. Baker (2003) did not find statistically significant results in seventh-grade students' knowledge of scientific method and attitudes toward science, but science fair attendance seemed to improve female participants' attitude and interest in science. A recent study by Brandeis University, commissioned by the FIRST Lego League 2008–2009, reported positive influences on youth participants' attitudes, skills, knowledge of science and technology, and self-confidence.

10. The FIRST Lego League is a partnership between FIRST (For Inspiration and Recognition of Science and Technology), an organization that was founded by inventor Dean Kamen in 1989, and the Lego Group, the company that sells Lego bricks and boxes. The league hosts international competitions with over twenty thousand teams in over seventy countries (see http://www.firstlegoleague.org).

11. See First Lego League (2008–2009).

12. J. H. Forrester (2010) found that participation in these public events, which often is encouraged by teachers and parents, is highly correlated with later career choices in STEM majors. Although girls initially participated in science fairs less frequently than boys, for the past twenty years their participation rate has been greater than that of boys. T. A. Greenfield (1995) found that boys have been and continue to be more likely than girls to prepare physical, earth, math, and computer science projects. A report of the FIRST Lego League 2008–2009 showed that robotics competitions have had only marginal success in increasing girls' participation. In academic year 2008–2009, 7,800 teams participated in the league robotics competition, and 70 percent youth participants were boys.

13. For an overview on benefits of learning robotics, see F. Baretto and V. Benitti (2012); for the relationship between robotics activities and science literacy, see Florence Sullivan (2008); and for the relationship to positive youth development, see Marina Bers's book *Designing Interactive Experiences for Positive Youth Development: From Playpen to Playground* (2012).

14. See Y. B. Kafai, W. Burke, and C. Mote (2012).

15. For a comprehensive overview of electronic textile construction kits, learning activities, and cultural issues, see *Textile Messages: Dispatches from the World of e-Textiles and Education*, edited by Leah Buechley, Kylie Peppler, Mike Eisenberg, and Yasmin Kafai (2013).

16. See Y. B. Kafai, E. Lee, K. A. Searle, D. A. Fields, E. Kaplan, and D. Lui (2014).

17. For a more extensive discussion on the value of transparency as an educational principle, see articles by L. Buechley (2010) and M. Eisenberg, A. Eisenberg, L. Buechley, and Elumeze Nwanua (2006).

18. More extensive discussions of cultural and gender differences in computing and crafting can be found in Y. B. Kafai and K. A. Peppler (2014), but see also Y. B. Kafai, D. Fields, and K. Searle (2012). An excellent historical examination on how programming became masculine can be found in Nathan Ensmenger (2010).

19. See Lars Spuybroek, *The Sympathy of Things: Ruskin and the Ecology of Design*, 53. Many thanks to Mike Eisenberg for locating and sharing this great quote.

20. See L. Buechley and B. Mako Hill (2010).

21. The design and research on e-crafting circles was conducted together with Orkan Telhan from Penn Design and Karen Elinich at The Franklin Institute.

22. See N. Rusk, M. Resnick, R. Berg, and M. Pezalla-Granlund (2008).

23. John Dewey (1938).

24. For more detail on shop classes for the next millennium and HyperGami designs, see Eisenberg and Eisenberg (1998). Mike Rose's book *The Mind at Work* (2004) provides excellent analyses of intellectual work in vocational trades. Amon Millner's Hook-Ups are described in his 2010 dissertation and in a 2009 chapter. The design studies with MaKey MaKey can be found in E. Lee, Y. B. Kafai, V. Vaseduvan. and R. L. Davis, and (2014). The Math on a Sphere project is described in more detail by Sherry Hsi and Mike Eisenberg (2012).

Chapter 7

1. See Seymour Papert, *The Children's Machine: Rethinking School in the Age of the Computer* (1993a, 1–2).

2. See http://www.rogerschank.com.

3. Like Jane Margolis, R. Estrella, J. Goode, J. J. Holme, and K. Nao (2008), we distinguish between computing education (courses that introduce programming into K–12 schools) and technology education (courses that teach word processing, Powerpoint, and other applications). Computer science encompasses a far wider range of concepts and practices than what is addressed in programming courses. We refer to computer science education when we talk about undergraduate education that is meant to be an introduction into the discipline.

4. Books on Scratch range from how-to guides to advanced texts that explore extensive activities that use the software. These include Mike Badger's *Scratch 1.4: Beginner's Guide*, LEAD's *Scratch Programming Adventure!*, J. L. Ford's *Scratch Programming for Teens*, Sylvia Martinez and Gary Stagers's *Invent to Learn*, and the ScratchEd website at http://scratched.media.mit.edu.

5. According to the U.S. Bureau of Labor Statistics (2012), jobs related to computer systems design are projected to grow nearly 50 percent by 2020. Employers have

trouble filling these jobs, however, and 65 percent of U.S. tech firms fill IT-related positions overseas.

6. See College Board (2012). In 2013, the number of students who took Advanced Placement tests in computer science increased nearly 25 percent, and the number of students enrolled in AP computer science courses increased 16 percent. The number of students enrolled in CS at PhD-granting institutions has jumped nearly 30 percent, marking an increase for five years in a row. This suggests that families are aware of the job reports, and students have the aptitude and interest.

7. For a syllabus (of a course that uses a Scratch-based language), see http://bjc .berkeley.edu.

8. C. Wilson, L. A. Sudol, C. Stephenson, and M. Stehlik (2010).

9. Currently, only ten U.S. states (most recently Washington state in July 2013) offer high school core credit (typically as a math or science) for a computer science course. The other 80 percent of U.S. states treat computer science as an elective. For a state-by-state analysis and more on getting computer science offered as a core curricula subject, see Computing in the Core at http://www.computinginthecore.org.

10. See also recent efforts by the United Kingdom Department of Education at https://www.gov.uk/government/publications/national-curriculum-in-england -computing-programmes-of-study.

11. J. Gal-Ezer, C. Beeri, D. Harel, and A. Yehudai (1995, 73).

12. For more info, see http://www.corestandards.org.

13. M. Johnson and J. L. Bookey (2012).

14. http://www.computinginthecore.org.

15. L. Cuban (2001).

16. For more information on learning with computers in afterschool and community technology centers, see M. Cole (2005) and B. Hirsch (2005). The design and evaluation of Computer Clubhouse network activities have been described in detail by Y. Kafai, K. A. Peppler, and R. Chapman (2009).

17. Dale Dougherty (2013, 8).

18. Ibid.

19. H. Jenkins (2010b).

20. Q. Burke and Y. B. Kafai (forthcoming).

21. Karen Brennan (2013, 187).

22. See C. Kelleher and R. Pausch (2005).

23. John Dewey (1915, 38).

24. Seymour Papert (1993b, 31).

25. John Dewey (1925, 10).

26. John Dewey and J. L. Childs (1933, 47).

27. Ibid., 61.

28. Douglas Rushkoff (2011).

29. See E. Larson (2013).

30. See Brookline.com, Beaver County Day School Profile, http://brookline.com/education-2/schools/private-schools/beaver-country-day-school.

31. Andrea Forte and Mark Guzdial (2004).

32. Papert (1993a, 217).

Chapter 8

1. See Lesley Chilcott's *Huffington Post* article "Code.org: Coding Is Not as Hard as You Think" at http://www.huffingtonpost.com/lesley-chilcott/computer-coding-classes_b_2778974.html.

2. Closing keynote presentation by Jane Margolis, "Unlocking the Clubhouse: A Decade Later and Now What?," delivered at the SIGCSE '13 conference in Denver, Colorado.

3. See Chilcott (2013).

4. See Jim Darby and James Catterall (1994), who argue for the arts (aRts) as the fourth R. See also Cathy Davidson's 2012 blog post, "Why We Need a Fourth R: Reading, wRiting, aRithmetic, algoRithms," at http://dmlcentral.net/blog/cathy-davidson/why-we-need-4th-r-reading-writing-arithmetic-algorithms.

5. In her 2007 and 2012 books, Marina Bers provides many examples of designing and learning in early childhood and younger grades. The programming tools Daisy the Dinosaur, Hopscotch, and Move the Turtle are available at the iTunes App store. The development of Scratch Jr. is funded by a National Science Foundation grant to Mitchel Resnick's MIT team and Marina Bers.

6. The design and development of the Quest to Learn school is described in a 2010 report by Katie Salen, R. Torres, L. Wolozin, R. Rugo-Tepper, and A. Shapiro. Descriptions and research on Globaloria's development can be found in R. Reynolds and M. Chiu's 2013 paper and at www.globaloria.org.

7. More about the design and research on the Exploring Computer Science curriculum can be found at www.exploringcs.org/curriculum, the ACM CS curriculum is available at Computer Science Teacher Association (2006), and descriptions of the Software Engineering Pilot program in New York City Schools can be found at C. Fadjo (2013) and in the press release from the New York City Public Schools at http://www.nyc.gov/portal/site/nycgov/menuitem.c0935b9a57bb4ef3daf2f1c701c7 89a0/index.jsp?pageID=mayor_press_release&catID=1194&doc_name=http%3A// www.nyc.gov/html/om/html/2013a/pr074-13.html&cc=unused1978&rc=1194& ndi=1.

8. See Margaret Honey and David Kanter's 2013 overview on maker activities as well as Sylvia Martinez and Gary Stager's 2013 compilation of maker and programming workshop activities.

9. See the 2011 National Research Council report on the general importance of informal learning places for science, the 2005 work by psychologist Barton Hirsch on the importance of community centers such as Boys and Girls Clubs, the 2009 book edited by Yasmin Kafai, Kylie A. Peppler, and Robbin Chapman on the Computer Clubhouse network, and the 2014 book edited by Brigid Barron, Kim Gomez, Nichole Pinkard, and Crystle K. Martin on digital media afterschool centers and youth media spaces in public libraries.

10. See more on connected play by Y. B. Kafai and D. Fields (2013).

11. The idea of "being digital" was foreshadowed in a collection of essays by Nicholas Negroponte (1995) published initially in *Wired* magazine.

12. Sherry Turkle (2011, 1).

13. See http://www.smh.com.au/digital-life/hometech/wikihouse-pioneers-doityour self-home-building-20130301-2f9xd.html.

14. See Margolis (2013).

15. In 1984, cultural psychologist Sylvia Scriber articulated these three purposes of literacy as she examined the roles of traditional literacies in relation to print, but they easily extend into the digital world.

16. Ibid.

References

Anderson, C. 2012. *Makers: The New Industrial Revolution*. New York: Crown Business.

Aragon, C., S. Poon, and A. Monroy-Hernández. 2009. A Tale of Two Communities: Fostering Collaboration and Creativity in Scientists and Children. In *Proceedings of the Seventh ACM Conference on Creativity and Cognition*, 9–18. New York: ACM.

Bader-Natal, A., A. Monroy-Hernández, J. D. Zamfirescu-Pereira, and S. Farnham. 2012. Meta-remix: Reflecting on Four Communities Built for Learning, Tinkering, and Remixing with Code. Paper presented at the Digital Media and Learning Conference, San Francisco, CA, March.

Badger, M. 2010. *Scratch 1.4: A Beginner's Guide*. Birmingham, UK: Packt Press.

Baretto, F., and V. Benitti. 2012. Exploring the Educational Potential of Robotics in Schools: A Systematic Review. *Computers & Education* 58:978–988.

Barron, B., K. Gomez, N. Pinkard, and C. K. Martin. 2014. *Cultivating Creative Production and Digital Citizenship in Urban Communities: The Digital Youth Network*. Cambridge, MA: MIT Press.

Benkler, Y. 2006. *The Wealth of Networks: How Social Production Transforms Markets and Freedom*. New Haven, CT: Yale University Press.

Bers, M. 2007. *From Blocks to Robots: Learning with Technology in the Early Childhood Classroom*. New York: Teachers College Press.

Bers, M. 2012. *Designing Digital Experiences for Positive Youth Development: From Playpen to Playground*. New York: Oxford University Press.

Black, R. 2008. *Adolescents and Online Fan Fiction*. New York: Lang.

Brand, S. 1988. *The Media Lab: Inventing the Future at MIT*. New York: Penguin Books.

Bransford, J., A. Brown, and R. Cocking. 2000. *How People Learn*. Washington, DC: National Academy Press.

Braught, G., L. M. Eby, and T. Wahls. 2008. The Effects of Pair-Programming on Individual Programming Skill. In *Proceedings of the Thirty-ninth SIGCSE Technical Symposium on Computer Science Education*, 200–204. New York: ACM.

Brennan, K. 2012. Best of Both Worlds: Issues of Structure and Agency in Computational Creation, in and out of School. PhD dissertation, Massachusetts Institute of Technology, Cambridge, MA.

Brennan, K., A. Monroy-Hernández, and M. Resnick. 2010. Making Projects, Making Friends: Online Communities as Catalyst for Interactive Media Creation. *New Directions for Youth Development* 128:75–83.

Brennan, K., and M. Resnick. 2012. New Frameworks for Studying and Assessing the Development of Computational Thinking. Paper presented at the Annual Meeting of the American Educational Research Association, Vancouver, April 2012.

Brookline.com. n.d. Beaver County Day School Profile. http://brookline.com/education-2/schools/private-schools/beaver-country-day-school.

Brown, J. S., A. Collins, and P. Duguid. 1989. Situated Cognition and the Culture of Learning. *Educational Researcher* 18:32–42.

Bruckman, A. 1997. MOOSE Crossing: Construction, Community, and Learning in a Networked Virtual World for Kids. PhD Dissertation, MIT Media Lab, Cambridge, MA.

Buechley, L. 2010. Questioning Invisibility. *IEEE Computer* 43 (4):84–86.

Buechley, L., and B. M. Hill. 2010. LilyPad in the Wild: How Hardware's Long Tail Is Supporting New Engineering and Design Communities. In *Proceedings of Designing Interactive Systems (DIS)*, 199–207. New York: ACM.

Buechley, L., K. A. Peppler, M. Eisenberg, and Y. B. Kafai, eds. 2013. *Textile Messages: Dispatches from the World of e-Textiles and Education.* New York: Lang.

Bureau of Labor Statistics. 2012. *Employment Projections 2010–2020.* http://www.bls.gov/emp/.

Burke, Q. 2012. The Workings of a New Pencil: Introducing Programming-as-Writing in the Middle School Classroom. *Journal of Media Literacy Education* 4 (2):121–135.

Burke, Q., and Y. B. Kafai. 2012. The Writers' Workshop for Youth Programmers. In *Proceedings of the Forty-third SIGCSE Technical Symposium on Computer Science Education*, 433–438. New York: ACM.

Calkins, L. M. 1986. *The Art of Teaching Writing.* Concord, Canada: Irwin Press.

Burke, Q., and Y. B. Kafai. 2014. DIY Zones for Scratch Designs in Class and Club. *International Journal of Learning and Media* 3 (4).

Cassell, J., and H. Jenkins, eds. 1998. *From Barbie to* Mortal Kombat*: Gender and Computer Games.* Cambridge, MA: MIT Press.

Cheliotis, G., and J. Yew. 2009. An Analysis of the Social Structure of Remix Culture. In *Proceedings of the Fourth International Conference on Communities and Technologies, University Park, PA, June 25–27,* 165–174. New York: ACM.

Chilcott, L., 2013, *What Most Schools Don't Teach.* YouTube Video . http://www .youtube.com/watch?v=nKIu9yen5nc.

Ching, C. C., and Y. B. Kafai. 2008. Peer Pedagogy: Student Collaboration and Reflection in Learning through Design. *Teachers College Record* 110 (12):2601–2632.

Clements, D. 1999. The Future of Educational Computing Research: The Case of Computer Programming. *Information Technology in Childhood Education Annual* 1:147–179.

Clements, D., and J. S. Meredith. 1993. Research on Logo: Effects and Efficacy. *Journal of Computing in Childhood Education* 4:263–290.

Clements, D., and J. Sarama. 1997. Research on Logo: A Decade of Progress. *Computers in the Schools* 14 (1–2):9–46.

Cohoon, J. M., and W. Asprey, eds. 2006. *Women and Information Technology: Research on Under-representation.* Cambridge, MA: MIT Press.

Cole, M. 2005. Cross-cultural and Historical Perspectives on the Developmental Consequences of Education. *Human Development* 48 (4):195–216.

College Board. 2012. College Board's Database of AP Course Audits. https://apcourseaudit.epiconline.org/ledger/search.php.

Collins, A., and R. Halverson. 2009. *Rethinking Education in the Age of Technology: The Digital Revolution and Schooling in America.* New York: Teachers College Press.

Computer Science Teacher Association. 2006. *A Model Curriculum for K–12 Computer Science.* 2nd ed. New York: ACM.

Cuban, L. 2001. *Oversold and Underused: Computers in the Classroom.* Cambridge, MA: Harvard University Press.

Darby, J., and J. Catterall. 1994. The Fourth R: The Arts and Learning. *Teachers College Record* 96 (2):299–328.

Davidson, C. 2012. Why We Need a Fourth R: Reading, wRiting, aRithmetic, algoRithms. http://dmlcentral.net/blog/cathy-davidson/why-we-need-4th-r-reading-writing -arithmetic-algorithms.

DeMarco, T., and T. Lister. 1999. *Peopleware: Productive Projects and Teams.* 2nd ed. New York: Dorset House.

Denner, J., and S. Campe. 2008. What Games by Girls Can Tell Us. In *Beyond Barbie and* Mortal Kombat: *New Perspectives on Gender and Gaming*, ed. Y. B. Kafai, C. Heeter, J. Denner, and J. Sun, 129–144. Cambridge, MA: MIT Press.

Denner, J., and L. Werner. 2007. Computer Programming in Middle School: How Pairs Respond to Challenges. *Journal of Educational Computing Research* 37 (2):131–150.

Dewey, J. 1915. *The School and Society*. Chicago: University of Chicago Press.

Dewey, J. 1925. *Experience and Nature*. In *John Dewey: The Later Works*. Vol. 1., ed. J. A. Boydston. Carbondale: Southern Illinois University Press.

Dewey, J. 1938. *Experience and Education*. New York: Simon & Schuster.

Dewey, J., and J. L. Childs. 1933. The Social-Economic Situation and Education. In *The Educational Frontier*, ed. W. H. Kilpatrick, 32–72. New York: Appleton-Century.

Dill, K. 2013. Game Design Badge: Boy Scouts Embrace the Digital World. *Inc.com*, March 8.

DiSalvo, B., M. Guzdial, T. McKlin, C. Meadows, K. Perry, C. Steward, and A. Bruckman. 2009. Glitch Game Testers: African American Men Breaking Open the Console. Paper presented at Breaking New Ground: Innovation in Games, Play, Practice and Theory, Digital Games Research Association (DiGRA), Brunel, UK, September.

diSessa, A. 2001. *Changing Minds: Computers, Learning and Literacy*. Cambridge, MA: MIT Press.

Dougherty, D. 2010. Teachers as Makers: Educators Discover How Hands-on Learning Can Help Teach Writing. O'Reilly Radar. Last modified 2010. http://radar.oreilly .com/2010/12/teachers-as-makers.html.

Dougherty, D. 2013. The Maker Mindset. In *Design, Make, Play: Growing the Next Generation of STEM Innovators*, ed. M. Honey and D. E. Kanter, 7–12. New York: Routledge.

Edwards, L. 1998. Embodying Mathematics and Science: Microworlds as Representations. *Journal of Mathematical Behavior* 17 (1):53–78.

Eisenberg, M., and A. Eisenberg. 1998. Shop Class for the Next Millennium: Education through Computer-Enriched Handicrafts. *Journal of Interactive Media in Education* 98 (8):1–30.

Eisenberg, M., A. Eisenberg, L. Buechley, and E. Nwanua. 2006. Invisibility Considered Harmful: Revisiting Traditional Principles of Ubiquitous Computing in the Context of Education. In *Proceedings of Fourth IEEE International Workshop on Wireless, Mobile and Ubiquitous Technology in Education (WMTE'06)*, 102–110. New York: IEEE.

Ensmenger, N. 2010. Making Programing Masculine. In *Gender Codes: Why Women Are Leaving Computing*, ed. T. J. Misa, 115–142. New York: Wiley.

Fadjo, C. 2013. A Comprehensive Software Engineering Education Program for Grades Six to Twelve in NYC Public Schools. In *Proceedings of the Forty-fourth ACM Technical Symposium of Computer Science Education*, ed. T. Camp and P. Tyman, 735. New York: ACM.

Feinberg, B. 2007. The Lucy Calkins Project: Parsing a Self-proclaimed Literacy Guru. *Education Next* 7 (3):27–32.

Feurzeig, W. 2010. Toward a Culture of Creativity: A Personal Perspective on Logo's Early Years and Ongoing Potential. *International Journal of Computers for Mathematical Learning* 15:257–265.

Fields, D. A., M. Giang, and Y. B. Kafai. 2013.Understanding Collaborative Practices in the Scratch Online Community: Patterns of Participation among Youth Designers. In *Proceedings of the Tenth International Conference of Computer Supported Collaborative Learning (CSCL 2013)*. Madison, WI: International Society of the Learning Sciences.

Fildes, J. 2007. Free Tool Offers "Easy" Coding. BBC News. Last modified May 14, 2007. http://news.bbc.co.uk/2/hi/technology/6647011.stm.

First Lego League. 2008–2009. *More Than Robots: An Evaluation of the FIRST Robotics Competitions Participant and Institutional Impacts*. Brandeis University, Center for Youth and Communities, Heller School for Social Policy and Management. http://www.usfirst.org/uploadedFiles/Who/Impact/Brandeis_Studies/FRC_eval_finalrpt.pdf.

Ford, J. L. 2008. *Scratch Programming for Teens*. Boston, MA: Course Technology.

Forrester, J. H. 2010. Competitive Science Events: Gender, Interest, Science Self-Efficacy, and Academic Major Choice. PhD dissertation, North Carolina University.

Forte, A., and M. Guzdial. 2004. Computers for Communication, not Calculation: Media as a Motivation and Context for Learning. In *Proceedings of the Thirty-seventh Annual Hawaii International Conference on System Sciences (HICSS'04)*. Manoa, HI: Shidley College of Business.

Fox, S., and M. Madden. 2006. Riding the Waves of "Web 2.0." Pew Internet & American Life Project. Last modified 2006. http://www.pewinternet.org/pdfs/PIP_Web_2.0.pdf.

Frauenfelder, M. 2011. *Made by Hand: Searching for Meaning in a Throwaway World*. New York: Portfolio Books.

Gal-Ezer, J., C. Beeri, D. Harel, and A. Yehudai. 1995. A High School Program in Computer Science. *Computer* 28 (10):73–80.

Games, A. 2012. Twenty-first-Century Language and Literacy in Gamestar Mechanic: Middle School Students' Appropriation through Play of the Discourse of Computer Game Designers. PhD dissertation, University of Wisconsin, Madison.

Gargarian, G. 1996. The Art of Design. In *Constructionism in Practice: Designing Thinking, and Learning in a Digital World*, ed. Y. B. Kafai and M. Resnick, 125–160. Mahwah, NJ: Erlbaum.

Gastwirth, J. L. 1972. The Estimation of the Lorenz Curve and Gini Index. *Review of Economics and Statistics* 54 (3):306–316.

Gauntlett, D. 2011. *Making Is Connecting: The Social Meaning of Creativity from DIY and Knitting to YouTube and Web 2.0.* Cambridge, UK: Polity Press.

Gee, J. 2003. *What Video Games Teach Us about Learning and Literacy.* New York: Palgrave.

Gershenfeld, N. 2007. *Fab: The Coming Revolution on Your Desktop: From Personal Computers to Personal Fabrication.* New York: Basic Books.

Goldberg, D. 2004. The Scratch Is Hip-Hop: Appropriating the Phonographic Medium. In *Appropriating Technology: Vernacular Science and Social Power*, ed. R. Eglash, J. Crossiant, G. Di Chiro, and R. Fouche, 107–144. Minneapolis: University of Minnesota Press.

Goldman-Segal, R. 1998. *Points of Viewing of Children's Thinking: A Digital Ethnographer's Journey.* Mahwah, NJ: Erlbaum.

González, N., L. Moll, and C. Amanti. 2005. *Funds of Knowledge: Theorizing Practices in Households, Communities, and Classrooms.* Mahweh, NJ: Erlbaum.

Greenfield, T. A. 1995. An Exploration of Gender Participation Patterns in Science Competitions. *Journal of Research in Science Teaching* 32 (7):735–748.

Griffin, J., E. Kaplan, Q. Burke, and Y. B. Kafai. 2010. Deconstruction Kits in Scratch: Designing Scratch Debugems for Learning Core Programming Concepts. Paper presented at the Forty-second SIGCSE Technical Symposium, Dallas, TX.

Grover, S., and R. Pea. 2013. Computational Thinking in K–12: A Review of the State of the Field. *Educational Researcher* 42 (2):59–69.

Guzdial, M. 2004a. Programming Environments for Novices. In *Computer Science Education Research*, ed. S. Fincher and M. Petre, 127–154. London: Taylor & Francis.

Guzdial, M. 2004b. Software-Realized Scaffolding to Facilitate Programming for Science Learning. *Interactive Learning Environments* 4 (1):1–44.

Guzzetti, B., K. Elliot, and D. Welsch. 2010. *DIY Media in the Classroom: New Literacies across Content Areas.* New York: Teachers College Press.

Guzzetti, B. J., and M. Gamboa. 2004. Zines for Social Justice: Adolescent Girls Writing on their Own. *Reading Research Quarterly* 39 (4): 408–436.

Harel, I. 1991. *Children Designers: Interdisciplinary Constructions for Learning and Knowing Mathematics in a Computer-Rich School*. Norwood, NJ: Ablex.

Harel, I., and S. Papert. 1990. Software Design as a Learning Environment. *Interactive Learning Environments* 1:1–32.

Harms, K. J., J. H. Kerr, M. Ichinco, M. Santolucito, A. Chuck, T. Koscik, M. Chou, and C. L. Kelleher. 2012. Designing a Community to Support Long-Term Interest in Programming for Middle School Children. In *Proceedings of the Eleventh International Conference on Interaction Design and Children*. New York: ACM.

Hayes, E. R., and I. A. Games. 2008. Making Computer Games and Design Thinking: A Review of Current Software and Strategies. *Games and Culture* 3 (4):309–322.

Heeter, C., and B. Winn. 2008. Gender Identity, Play Style and Design of Games for Classroom Learning. In *Beyond Barbie and* Mortal Kombat: *New Perspectives on Gender and Gaming*, ed. Y. Kafai, C. Heeter, J. Denner, and J. Sun, 281–302. Cambridge, MA: MIT Press.

Hill, B. Mako, and A. Monroy-Hernández. 2013. The Remixing Dilemma: The Tradeoff between Generativity and Originality. *American Behavioral Scientist* 57 (5):643–663.

Hill, B. Mako, A. Monroy-Hernández, and K. Olson. 2010. Responses to Remixing on a Social Media Sharing Website. In *Proceedings of the Fourth International AAAI Conference on Weblogs and Social Media*, 74–81. Menlo Park, CA: AAAI.

Hirsch, B. 2005. *A Place to Call Home: After-School Programs for Urban Youth*. Washington, DC: American Psychological Association.

Holloway, S., and G. Valentine. 2003. *Cyberkids: Children in the Information Age*. London: Routledge Falmer.

Honey, M., and D. Kanter, eds. 2013. *Design, Make, Play: Growing the Next Generation of STEM Innovators*. New York: Routledge.

Hoyles, C., and R. Noss. 1990. *Windows of Meaning*. Dordrecht, Netherlands: Kluwer Academic Press.

Hsi, S., and M. Eisenberg. 2012. Math on a Sphere: Using Public Displays to Support Children's Creativity and Computational Thinking on 3D Surfaces. In *Proceedings of the Eleventh International Conference on Interaction Design and Children*. New York: ACM.

Ito, M., S. Baumer, and M. Bittanti. d. boyd, R. Cody, B. Herr, H. A. Horst, P. G. Lange, D. Mahendran, K. Martinez, C. J. Pascoe, D. Perkel, L. Robinson, C. Sims, and

L. Tripp. 2009. *Hanging Out, Messing Around, and Geeking Out: Living and Learning with New Media*. Cambridge, MA: MIT Press.

Ito, M., K. Gutiérrez, S. Livingstone, B. Penuel, J. Rhodes, K. Salen, J. Schor, J. Sefton-Green, and S. C. Watkins. 2013. *Connected Learning: An Agenda for Research and Design*. Irvine, CA: Digital Media and Learning Research Hub.

James, C., with K. Davis, A. Flores, J. M. Francis, L. Pettingill, M. Rundle, and H. Gardner. 2009. *Young People, Ethics, and the New Digital Media: A Synthesis from the GoodPlay Project*. Cambridge, MA: MIT Press.

Jayadevappa, S., and R. Shankar. 2009. The Changing Ways of Computer Science and Engineering Education. Paper presented at the ASEE Annual Conference and Exposition, Austin, TX, June.

Jenkins, H. 2010a. *Afterword to DIY Media: Creating, Sharing and Learning with New Technologies*. Edited by M. Knobel and C. Lankshear. New York: Lang.

Jenkins, H. 2010b. Is New Media Incompatible with Schooling? An Interview with Rich Halverson. Accessed April 1, 2010. http://henryjenkins.org/2010/03/is_new_media_incompatable_with.html.

Jenkins, H., K. Clinton, R. Purushotma, A. Robison, and M. Weigel. 2006. *Confronting the Challenges of Participatory Culture: Media Education for the Twenty-first Century*. Chicago: MacArthur Foundation.

Johnson, M., and J. L. Bookey. 2012. The Common Core Must Include Computer Science. *Huffington Post*. Accessed September 20, 2013. http://www.huffingtonpost.com/maggie-johnson/common-corestandards_b_2258882.html.

Jones, M. C. 2010. Reuse of Source Code in Software Production. PhD dissertation, University of Illinois.

Kafai, Y. B. 1995. *Minds in Play: Computer Game Design as a Context for Children's Learning*. Mahwah, NJ: Erlbaum.

Kafai, Y. B. 1996. Gender Differences in Children's Constructions of Video Games. In *Interacting with Video*, ed. P. M. Greenfield and R. R. Cocking, 39–66. Norwood, NJ: Ablex.

Kafai, Y. B. 1998. Video Game Designs by Children: Consistency and Variability of Gender Differences. In *From Barbie to* Mortal Kombat*: Gender and Computer Games*, ed. J. Cassell and H. Jenkins, 90–114. Cambridge, MA: MIT Press.

Kafai, Y. B., W. Burke, and C. Mote. 2012. What Makes Things Fun to Participate? The Role of Audience for Middle School Game Designers. In *Proceedings of the Eleventh International Interaction Design and Children Conference*. New York: ACM.

Kafai, Y. B., and C. C. Ching. 2001. Affordances of Collaborative Software Design Planning for Elementary Students' Science Talk. *Journal of the Learning Sciences* 10 (3):323–363.

Kafai, Y. B., and D. Fields. 2013. *Connected Play: Tweens in a Virtual World*. Cambridge, MA: MIT Press.

Kafai, Y. B., D. A. Fields, and W. Q. Burke. 2010. Entering the Clubhouse: Case Studies of Young Programmers Joining Scratch Community. *Journal of Organizational and End User Computing* 22 (2):21–35.

Kafai, Y. B., D. A. Fields, R. Roque, W. Q. Burke, and A. Monroy-Hernández. 2012. Collaborative Agency in Youth Online and Offline Creative Production in Scratch. *Research and Practice in Technology Enhanced Learning* 7 (2):63–87.

Kafai, Y. B., D. Fields, and K. Searle. 2012. Making Learning Visible: Connecting Crafts, Circuitry, and Coding in e-textile Designs. In *Proceedings of the Tenth International Conference of the Learning Sciences (ICLS 2012)*, 188–195. Atlanta, GA: ICLS.

Kafai, Y. B., C. Heeter, J. Denner, and J. Y. Sun, eds. 2008. *Beyond Barbie and* Mortal Kombat*: New Perspectives on Gender and Gaming*. Cambridge, MA: MIT Press.

Kafai, Y. B., E. Lee, K. A. Searle, D. A. Fields, E. Kaplan, and D. Lui. 2014. A Crafts-Oriented Approach to Computing in High School: Introducing Computational Concepts, Practices, and Perspectives with Electronic Textiles. *Transactions on Computing Education* 14 (1):1–20.

Kafai, Y. B., and K. A. Peppler. 2011. Youth, Technology and DIY: Developing Participatory Competencies in Creative Media Production. *Review of Research in Education* 35:89–119.

Kafai, Y. B., and K. A. Peppler. 2014. Transparency Reconsidered: Creative, Critical, and Connected Making with E-textiles. In *Critical DIY: Critical Making and Social Media*, ed. M. Ratto and M. Boler. Cambridge, MA: MIT Press.

Kafai, Y., K. A. Peppler, and R. Chapman, eds. 2009. *The Computer Clubhouse. Creativity and Constructionism in Youth Communities*. New York: Teachers College Press.

Kafai, Y. B., K. A. Peppler, and G. Chiu. 2007. High-Tech Programmers in Low-Income Communities: Seeding Reform in a Community Technology Center. In *Communities and Technologies*, ed. C. Steinfield, B. Pentland, M. Ackerman, and N. Contractor, 545–564. New York: Springer.

Kafai, Y. B., and M. Resnick. 1996. *Constructionism in Practice*. Mahwah, NJ: Erlbaum.

Kafai, Y. B., and M. Roberts. 2002. On Becoming Junior Software Designers. In *Proceedings of the Fifth International Conference on the Learning Sciences*, ed. R. Steevens and P. Bell, 191–198. Mahwah, NJ: Erlbaum .

Kafai, Y. B., K. Searle, E. Kaplan, D. Fields, E. Lee, and D. Lui. 2012. Cupcake Cushions, Scooby Doo Shirts, and Soft Boomboxes: E-textiles in High School to Promote Computational Concepts, Practices, and Perceptions. In *Proceedings of the Forty-fourth*

SIGCSE Technical Symposium on Computer Science Education, 311–316. New York: ACM.

Kay, A., and A. Goldberg. 1977. Personal Dynamic Media. *Computer* 10 (3):31–41.

Kelleher, C., and R. Pausch. 2005. Lowering the Barriers to Programming: A Taxonomy of Programming Environments and Languages for Novice Programmers. *ACM Computing Surveys* 37 (2):83–137.

Knobel, M., and C. Lankshear. 2010. *DIY Media: Creating, Sharing and Learning with New Technologies*. New York: Lang.

Lankshear, C., and M. Knobel. 2008. Remix: The Art and Craft of Endless Hybridization. *Journal of Adolescent & Adult Literacy* 52 (1):22–33.

Larson, E. 2013. Coding the Curriculum. *Mashable*. Accessed September 25, 2013. http://mashable.com/2013/09/22/coding-curriculum.

Lave, J. 1988. *Cognition in Practice: Mind, Mathematics and Culture in Everyday Life*. New York: Cambridge University Press.

Lave, J., and E. Wenger. 1991. *Situated Learning: Legitimate Peripheral Participation*. Cambridge, UK: Cambridge University Press.

Lee, E., Y. B. Kafai, V. Vasudevan, and R. L. Davis. 2014. Playing in the Arcade: Making Tangible Interfaces with MaKey MaKey for Scratch Games. In *Playful User Interfaces*, ed. A. Nijholt. New York: Springer.

LEAD (Learning through Engineering, Art, and Design) Group. 2012. *The Super Scratch Programming Adventure: Learn to Program by Making Cool Games*. San Francisco, CA: No Starch Press.

Lenhart, A. 2007. Cyberbullying. Pew Internet & American Life Project. Last modified 2007. http://pewinternet.org/Reports/2007/Cyberbullying/1-Findings.aspx.

Lessig, L. 2008. *Remix: Making Art and Commerce Thrive in a Hybrid Economy*. New York: Penguin Press.

Luther, K., and A. Bruckman. 2011. Leadership and Success Factors in Online Creative Collaboration. *IEEE Potentials* (September/October):27–32. http://pipeline.cc .gatech.edu/pdf/Luther-Bruckman-Potentials.pdf.

Luther, K., K. Caine, K. Ziegler, and A. Bruckman. 2011. Why It Works (When It Works): Success Factors in Online Creative Collaboration. In *GROUP '10: Proceedings of the ACM Conference on Supporting Group Work*, 1–10. New York: ACM Press.

Magnifico, A. M. 2010. Writing for Whom? Cognition, Motivation, and a Writer's Audience. *Educational Psychologist* 45 (3):167–184.

Maloney, J., L. Burd, Y. Kafai, N. Rusk, B. Silverman, and M. Resnick. 2004. Scratch: A Sneak Preview. In *C5 '04: Proceedings of the Second International Conference on Creat-*

ing, Connecting and Collaborating through Computing, 104–109. Washington, DC: IEEE Computer Society.

Manovich, L. 2005. Remix and Remixability. Last modified 2005. Accessed August 23, 2011. http://imlportfolio.usc.edu/ctcs505/manovichremixmodular.pdf.

Margolis, J. 2013. Unlocking the Clubhouse: A Decade Later and Now What? Closing keynote paper presented at the Forty-fourth ACM Technical Symposium of Computer Science Education, Denver, CO.

Margolis, J., and A. Fisher. 2002. *Unlocking the Clubhouse: Women in Computing*. Cambridge, MA: MIT Press.

Margolis, J., R. Estrella, J. Goode, J. J. Holme, and K. Nao. 2008. *Stuck in the Shallow End: Education, Race, and Computing*. Cambridge, MA: MIT Press.

Marshall, S. 2000. Planning in Context. PhD dissertation, University of California, Los Angeles.

Martin, F. 1996. Ideal and Real Systems: A Study of Notions of Control in Undergraduates Who Design Robots. In *Constructionism in Practice*, ed. Y. Kafai and M. Resnick, 255–268. Mahwah, NJ: Erlbaum.

Martin, F. 2001. *Robotic Explorations: A Hands-on Introduction to Engineering*. New York: Prentice Hall.

Martinez, S., and G. Stager. 2013. *Invent to Learn*. Torrance, CA: Constructing Modern Knowledge.

Millner, A. 2009. Interface Design with Hook Ups. In *The Computer Clubhouse: Constructionism and Creativity in Youth Communities*, ed. Y. Kafai, K. A. Peppler, and R. Chapman, 58–70. New York: Teachers College Press.

Millner, A. 2010. Computer as Chalk: Cultivating and Sustaining Communities of Youth as Designers of Tangible User Interfaces. PhD dissertation, Massachusetts Institute of Technology, Cambridge, MA.

Mills, K. A. 2010. A Review of the "Digital Turn" in the New Literacy Studies. *Review of Educational Research* 80 (2):246–271.

Monroy-Hernández, A. 2012. Designing for Remixing: Supporting an Onlne Community of Amateur Creators. PhD dissertation, Massachusetts Institute of Technology, Cambridge, MA.

Monroy-Hernández, A., and B. M. Hill. 2010. Cooperation and Attribution in an Online Community of Young Creators. Poster session presented at the ACM Conference on Computer Supported Collaborative Work (CSCW '10), Savannah, GA.

Monroy-Hernández, A., B. M. Hill, J. Gonzalez-Rivero, and d. boyd. 2011. Computers Can't Give Credit: How Automatic Attribution Falls Short in an Online Remixing

Community. In *Proceedings of the 2011 Annual Conference on Human Factors in Computing Systems*, 3421–3430. Aarhus, Denmark: Interaction Design Foundation.

Monroy-Hernández, A., and M. Resnick. 2008. Empowering Kids to Create and Share Programmable Media. *Interaction* 15 (2):50–53.

National Research Council, Computer Science and Telecommunications Board (CSTB). 2010. *Report of a Workshop on the Scope and Nature of Computational Thinking.* Washington, DC: National Academy Press.

National Research Council, Computer Science and Telecommunications Board (CSTB). 2011. *Report of a Workshop on Pedagogical Aspects of Computational Thinking.* Washington, DC: National Academy Press.

Negroponte, N. 1995. *Being Digital.* New York: Knopf.

Nickerson, J. V., and A. Monroy-Hernández. 2012. Appropriation and Creativity: User-Initiated Contests in Scratch. In *Proceedings of the Forty-fourth Hawaii International Conference on System Sciences*, 1–10. Manoa, HI: Shidley College of Business.

Noss, R., and C. Hoyles. 1996. *Windows on Mathematical Meanings: Learning Cultures and Computers.* Dordrecht, Netherlands: Kluwer Academic.

O'Reilly, T. 2005. What Is Web 2.0? Last modified 2005. http://www.ttivanguard .com/ttivanguard_cfmfiles/pdf/dc05/dc05session4003.pdf.

Palumbo, D. 1990. Programming Language/Problem-solving Research: A Review of Relevant Issues. *Review of Educational Research* 45:65–89.

Papert, S. 1975. *Some Poetic and Social Criteria for Education Design.* Cambridge, MA: MIT Press.

Papert, S. 1990. Computer Criticism vs. Technocentric Thinking. *Educational Researcher* 16 (1): 22–30.

Papert, S. 1991. Situating Constructionism. In *Constructionism*, ed. I. Harel and S. Papert, 111–130. Norwood, NJ: Ablex.

Papert, S. 1993a. *The Children's Machine: Rethinking School in the Age of the Computer.* New York: Basic Books.

Papert, S. 1993b. *Mindstorms: Children, Computers, and Powerful Ideas.* 2nd ed. New York: Basic Books. Originally published in 1980.

Papert, S. 1996. *The Connected Family: Bridging the Digital Generation Gap.* New York: Taylor Trade.

Papert, S. 1997. Tinkering towards Utopia: A Century of Public School Reform. *Journal of the Learning Sciences* 6 (4):417–427.

Papert, S. 2002. Hard Fun. *Bangor Daily News.* Last modified 2002. http://www .papert.org/articles/HardFun.html.

Papert, S., and I. Harel. 1991. *Situating Constructionsim*. Norwood, NJ: Ablex.

Parnas, D. 1972. On the Criteria to Be Used in Decomposing Systems into Modules. *Communications of the ACM* 15 (12):1053–1058.

Pea, R., and M. Kurland. 1984. On the Cognitive Effects of Learning Computer Programming. *New Ideas in Psychology* 2 (2):137–168.

Pea, R. D., and D. M. Kurland. 1983. *Logo Programming and the Development of Planning Skills*. New York: Bank Street College.

Pelletier, C. 2008. Gaming in Context: How Young People Construct Their Gendered Identities in Playing and Making Games. In *Beyond Barbie and Mortal Kombat: New Perspectives on Gender and Computer Games*, ed. Y. B. Kafai, C. Heeter, J. Denner, and J. Sun, 145–160. Cambridge, MA: MIT Press.

Peppler, K. A., and Y. B. Kafai. 2007. From SuperGoo to Scratch: Exploring Creative Digital Media Production in Informal Learning. *Learning, Media and Technology* 32 (2):149–166.

Perkel, D. 2008. "No, I Don't Feel Complimented": A Young Artist's Take on Copyright. Digital Youth Research. Last modified 2008. http://digitalyouth.ischool .berkeley.edu/node/105.html.

Perkins, D. N. 1986. *Knowledge as Design*. Hillsdale, NJ: Erlbaum.

Perrott, E. 2011. Copyright in the Classroom: Why Comprehensive Copyright Education Is Necessary in United States K–12 Education Curriculum. American University Intellectual Property Brief. Last modified 2011. http://digitalcommons.wcl. american.edu.

Prensky, M. 2001. Digital Natives, Digital Immigrants. *On the Horizon* 9 (5): 1–6.

Prensky, M. 2008. Programming Is the New Literacy. *Edutopia*. Last modified 2008. http://edutopia.org/literacy-computer-programming.

Ratto, M., and M. Boler, eds. 2014. *DIY Citizenship: Critical Making and Social Media*. Cambridge, MA: MIT Press.

Repenning, A., and A. Ioannidou. 2008. Broadening Participation through Scalable Game Design. In *SIGCSE '08 Proceedings of the Thirty-ninth SIGCSE Technical Symposium on Computer Science Education*, 305–309. New York: ACM.

Resnick, L. 1987. *Education and Learning to Think*. Washington, DC: National Academy Press.

Resnick, M. 1991. New Paradigms for Computing, New Paradigms for Thinking. In *Constructionism in Practice*, ed. Y. Kafai and M. Resnick, 255–268. Mahwah, NJ: Erlbaum.

Resnick, M. 1993. Behavior Construction Kits. *Communications of the ACM* 36 (7):64–71.

Resnick, M. 2012. Mother's Day, Warrior Cats, and Digital Fluency: Stories from the Scratch Online Community. Paper presented at the Constructionism 2012 Conference, August 21–25, Athens, Greece.

Resnick, M., J. Maloney, A. M. Hernández, N. Rusk, E. Eastmond, K. Brennan, A. D. Millner, et al. 2009. Scratch: Programming for Everyone. *Communications of the ACM* 52 (11):60–67.

Resnick, M., F. Martin, R. Sargent, and B. Silverman. 1996. Programmable Bricks: Toys to Think With. *IBM Systems Journal* 35 (3–4):443–452.

Resnick, M., and S. Ocko. 1991. Lego/Logo: Learning through and about Design. In *Constructionism*, ed. I. Harel and S. Papert, 141–150. Norwood, NJ: Erlbaum.

Resnick, M., and B. Silverman. 2005. Some Reflections on Designing Construction Kits for Kids. In *Proceedings of the 2005 Conference on Interaction Design and Children*, 117–122. New York: ACM.

Resnick, M., and U. Wilensky. 1998. Diving into Complexity: Developing Probabilistic Decentralized Thinking through Role-playing Activities. *Journal of the Learning Sciences* 7 (2): 153–172.

Reynolds, R., and M. Chiu. 2013. Formal and Informal Context Factors as Contributors to Student Engagement in a Guided Discovery-based Program of Game Design Learning. *Learning, Media, and Technology* 38 (4):429–462.

Rideout, V., U. Foehr, and D. Roberts. 2010. *Generation M2: Media in the Lives of 8- to 18-Year-Olds*. Menlo Park, CA: Kaiser Family Foundation.

Robbins, A., J. Rountree, and N. Rountree. 2003. Learning and Teaching Programming: A Review and Discussion. *Computer Science Education* 13 (2):137–172.

Roque, R. 2012. Making Together: Creative Collaboration for Everyone. Master's thesis, Massachusetts Institute of Technology, Cambridge, MA.

Rose, M. 2004. *The Mind at Work*. New York: Penguin.

Rushkoff, D. 2011. *Program or Be Programmed? Ten Commands for a Digital Age* New York: Soft Skull Press.

Rusk, N., M. Resnick, R. Berg, and M. Pezalla-Granlund. 2008. New Pathways into Robotics: Strategies for Broadening Participation. *Journal of Science Education and Technology* 17 (1):59–69.

Salen, K., R. Torres, L. Wolozin, R. Rufo-Tepper, and A. Shapiro. 2010. *Quest to Learn*. Cambridge, MA: MIT Press.

Salomon, G., and D. N. Perkins. 1987. Transfer of Cognitive Skills from Programming: When and How? *Journal of Educational Computing Research* 3:149–169.

Sawyer, K. 2007. *Group Genius: The Creative Power of Collaboration.* New York: Basic Books.

Scardamalia, M. 2002. Collective Cognitive Responsibility for the Advancement of Knowledge. In *Liberal Education in a Knowledge Society,* ed. B. Smith, 67–98. Chicago: Open Court.

Schön, D. A. 1983. *The Reflective Practitioner: How Professionals Think in Action.* New York: Basic Books.

Scribner, S. 1984. Literacy in Three Metaphors. *American Journal of Education* 93 (1):6–21.

Sfard, A. 1998. On Two Metaphors for Learning and the Dangers of Choosing Just One. *Educational Researcher* 26 (2):4–13.

Shaffer, D., and M. Resnick. 1999. Think Authenticity: New Media and Authentic Learning. *Journal of Interactive Learning Research* 10 (2):195–215.

Shirky, C. 2010. *Cognitive Surpluses: Creativity and Generosity in the Connected Age.* New York: Penguin Press.

Silver, J., E. Rosenbaum, and D. Shaw. 2012. MaKey MaKey: Improvising Tangible and Nature-based User Interfaces. In *Proceedings of the Sixth International Conference on Tangible, Embedded and Embodied Interaction,* 367–370. New York: ACM.

Simon, H. 1981. *The Sciences of the Artificial.* Cambridge, MA: MIT Press.

Soloway, E., and J. Spohrer. 1990. *Empirical Studies of Novice Programmers.* Norwood, NJ: Ablex.

Spencer, A. 2005. *DIY: The Rise of Lo-fi Culture.* London: Marion Boyars.

Spuybroek, L. 2012. *The Sympathy of Things: Ruskin and the Ecology of Design.* Rotterdam, The Netherlands: NAi Publishers.

Squire, K. 2011. *Video Games and Learning: Teaching and Participatory Culture in the Digital Age.* New York: Teachers College Press.

Streefland, L. 1991. *Fractions in Realistic Mathematics Education: A Paradigm of Developmental Research.* Dordrecht, Netherlands: Kluwer.

Sullivan, F. 2008. Robotics and Science Literacy: Thinking Skills, Science Process Skills, and Systems Understanding. *Journal of Research in Science Teaching* 45 (3):373–394.

Sutton, R. E. 1991. Equity and Computers. *Review of Educational Research* 61 (4):474–501.

Taylor, R. P., ed. 1980. *The Computer in School: Tutor, Tool, Ttutee*. New York: Teachers College Press.

Thagard, P. 2012. *The Cognitive Science of Science*. Cambridge, MA: MIT Press.

Thomas, M., ed. 2011. *Deconstructing Digital Natives: Young People, Technology, and the New Literacies*. New York: Routledge Press.

Turkle, S. 1984. *Second Self: Computers and the Human Spirit*. New York: Simon & Schuster.

Turkle, S. 1995. *Life on the Screen: Identity in the Age of the Internet*. New York: Simon & Schuster.

Turkle, S. 2007. *Evocative Objects: Things We Think With*. Cambridge, MA: MIT Press.

Turkle, S. 2011. *Alone Together: Why We Expect More from Technology and Less from Each Other*. New York: Basic Books.

Turkle, S., and S. Papert. 1991. Epistemological Pluralism and the Revaluation of the Concrete. In *Constructionism*, ed. I. Harel and S. Papert, 161–191. Norwood, NJ: Ablex.

von Hippel, E. 2005. *Democratizing Innovation*. Cambridge, MA: MIT Press.

Warschauer, M., and T. Matuchniak. 2010. New Technology and Digital Worlds: Analyzing Evidence of the Equity in Access, Use and Outcomes. *Review of Research in Education* 34 (1):179–225.

Webb, N. 1980. A Process-Outcome Analysis of Learning in Group and Individual Settings. *Educational Psychologist* 15:69–83.

Wenger, E. 2004. Communities of Practice: A Brief Introduction. Last modified 2004. http://www.ewenger.com/theory.

Wilensky, U. 1991. Abstract Meditations on the Concrete and Concrete Implications for Mathematics Education. In *Constructionism*, ed. Idit Harel and Seymour Papert, 193–204. Norwood, NJ: Ablex.

Williams, S. M. 2009. The Impact of Collaborative, Scaffolded learning in K–12 Schools: A Meta-Analysis." The Metiri Group and Cisco Systems. Last modified 2009. https://www.cisco.com/web/about/citizenship/socio-economic/docs/Metiri_Classroom_Collaboration_Research.pdf.

Williams, L., R. R. Kessler, W. Cunningham, and R. Jeffries. 2000. Strengthening the Case for Pair Programming. *IEEE Software* 17 (4):19–25.

Wilson, C., L.A. Sudol, C. Stephenson, and M. Stehlik. 2010. *Running on Empty: The Failure to Teach K–12 Computer Science in the Digital Age*. New York: ACM.

Wing, J. M. 2006. Computational Thinking. *Communications of the ACM* 49 (3):33–35.

Wing, J. M. 2010. Computational Thinking: What and Why? Last modified 2010. Accessed March 20, 2013. http://www.cs.cmu.edu/~CompThink/resources/TheLink Wing.pdf.

Wolber, D., H. Abelson, E. Spertus, and L. Looney. 2011. *App Inventor: Create Your Own Android Apps.* Sebastopol, CA: O'Reilly Media.

Wolf, M. 2008. *The Video Game Explosion: A History from Pong to Playstation and Beyond.* Westport, CT: Greenwood Press.

Yasar, S., and D. Baker. 2003. The Impact of Involvement in a Science Fair on Seventh-Grade Students. Paper presented at the Annual Meeting of the National Association for Research in Science Teaching, Philadelphia, PA, March.

Zagal, J. P., and A. Bruckman. 2005. From Samba Schools to Computer Clubhouses: Cultural Institutions as Learning Environments. *Convergence* 11:88–105.

Zhang, J., M. Scardamalia, R. Reeve, and R. Messina. 2009. Designs for Collective Cognitive Responsibility in Knowledge Building Communities. *Journal of the Learning Sciences* 18 (1):7–44.

Index